Chasing Kites

*One Mother's Unexpected
Journey Through Infertility,
Adoption, and Foster Care*

RACHEL MCCRACKEN

Chasing Kites
—— publishing ——

Copyright © 2017 Rachel McCracken
Chasing Kites: One Mother's Unexpected Journey Through Infertility, Adoption, and Foster Care

ISBN-10 (Ebook):   0-9997356-0-8
ISBN-13 (Ebook):   978-0-9997356-0-2
ISBN-13 (Paperback): 978-0999735619

Contents

Introduction 1

Chapter One: Beginnings 5

Chapter Two: A Family Begins. 29

Chapter Three: Coming Home. 57

Chapter Four: Molecular Moments 73

Chapter Five: Henry 99

Chapter Six: In-vitro Makes an Entrance 111

Chapter Seven: Adoption Is Not the Same . . .141

Epilogue 153

Acknowledgments 159

About the Author 161

Dedication

For my ever-devoted husband, Adam. This is your story too. Thank you for always opening your arms wide and loving without apology. Your approving smile and steady kindness continue to rescue me every single day. I would free rappel into a three-hundred-foot sinkhole for you!

And for my children, Daniel, Ezzy, Nikki, Juan, Jo Jo, Brian, Annie, and Hannah. You each uniquely bless our family and this world. Thank you for always being up for another crazy adventure, for letting me into your hearts, for allowing me to share *your* story, and for always helping Just One More.

Introduction

A few years ago, I was out hiking with a group of girlfriends in Washington State. We had all of our children in tow, about 30 or so. My oldest, Daniel, was carrying our youngest on his back. My second oldest, Ezzy, was helping my six-year-old navigate the loose rock up the path. My other kids were far up ahead herding my friends' small children onward, entertaining them along the way. It was one of those moments in time when I looked up, the summer sun glimmering off the mountains, a gentle summer breeze singing in the air with small squeals of laughter bouncing through the canyon, and I couldn't help but think, "Life is good!" As we were slogging up the steep rocky incline, my friend, Britteny, looked up and said, "Rach, I think we all have it wrong; you are the genius." I couldn't figure out what she meant. She continued, "Look at your kids. I think everyone should start with an older child!" I thought to myself, "you know what—she's right!"

My friends and family often tease that we have done everything backward, an unconventional road through parenthood. We did not start with one child, we started with four. We did not start with a baby, we started with older kids. We did not use fertility treatments to try to get pregnant first, we jumped straight into an international sibling adoption. Yes, it is unconventional, but it is also straight up awesome! In a few short years we built a little tribe that could immediately enjoy backpacking adventures, play school sports, start music lessons, even help with chores—the things we would have waited years for, or maybe a lifetime, if we had put all of our eggs in the fertility-treatment basket. It is not the right choice for everyone, but it was definitely the right choice for us.

It is hard to believe that one crazy adoption adventure beginning in Bogotá, Colombia, a decade ago has landed me here. I currently have four high schoolers, two awkward middle schoolers, a pretty little fifth grader, and a four-year-old who thinks she runs the house. All of this was accomplished in just eight short years. Crazy, exhausting, frustrating at times—and yet, I wouldn't change a single moment, a single decision, or a single opportunity.

Is adopting hard? Yes. Do I have bad days? Of course! Who doesn't? In an effort to create a family,

Adam and I have tackled adoption, foster care, and fertility treatments. We have experienced multiple miscarriages, lost adoption placements, returned foster babies, and failed fertility rounds. Heck, we have even experienced an eight-week stay in the neonatal unit with our IVF baby, and if we were given the chance to start over, to do it differently, we would not take it. The purpose-driven life we have created with our children is worth more than anything to us. It is actually everything!

Growing a successful family requires massive amounts of intentionality. It takes drive. It takes commitment. It is not for the faint of heart, but it is definitely for those who have a heart full of love and purpose. Parenting is messy, chaotic, and ugly at times (even in the very best families), but it is also joyful, rewarding, and downright amazing. If you are struggling to start a family, blend a family, or improve the family dynamic you already have, come along beside me as I share my family's journey and the things I have learned throughout it—purpose-driven principles that make life worth living and parenting worth doing.

CHAPTER ONE

Beginnings

I t was early March 2005 when we had just found
out we were expecting a baby, on my birthday,
which seemed serendipitous since Adam, my
husband, and I both have March birthdays. I was
twenty-nine, married to the best guy on the planet,
enjoying my teaching career, and now expecting
a baby. March gleefully skipped through time, my
life's plan in full swing. Just the way I had scheduled it.

While Adam was away canyoneering for his
birthday, I was off to dinner at a friend's celebrating
our successes when it began. Bleeding, cramping,
fainting; my first miscarriage came on fast and furious. This could not be happening! I tried really hard
not to spin my miscarriage suspicions into an over-
reaction that evening. Little did I know that first

pregnancy loss was a foreshadowing of things to come. The friends I was dining with were support-ive and positive, but what did any of us know about miscarriage, or even pregnancy, for that matter? We were all young with no children yet, future dreams of perfect families brightly shining before us.

I was only seven weeks along, but it felt like seven months when I realized this pregnancy would not be. Thankfully, I had planned to stay with Adam's parents that night. I was a total mess by the time I arrived at their house. I asked Adam's mom, Debbi, to take me to the emergency room, which was a complete rookie mistake, but again, what did I know back then? What were the emergency room doctors going to do for a seven-week pregnancy? Lovingly, Adam's mom did what I asked, and we sat in the cold, stark waiting area for hours. The pain was excruciating. Once I was finally seen, they could not ultrasound me because the hospital equipment was not sophisticated enough to produce images that early in a pregnancy. I was instructed to see my doctor the following week. So I waited. I waited for Adam to come home. I waited for Monday to come. And I waited to pass the pregnancy.

I was twenty-eight when Adam and I married. We desperately wanted a large family, which for us meant at least five kids, so we expected and planned that I would spend the next several years pregnant, adopting after I had the babies I could. Although grief-stricken, we lost our first little baby with no thought of future problems. For some irrational reason, I kept my first pregnancy test for several years, through several moves and several tearful nights.

At first, I kept that silly pregnancy test as a symbol of the family we were working to create. I thought I would toss it once we were safely into the second trimester of our next pregnancy, but the coveted twelve-week pregnancy status never materialized. Not for us. A second pregnancy did occur a few months later but never yielded a second trimester, or a third. And I still could not throw that lousy first pregnancy test away.

We were initially excited for this second chance at a baby. There was no need to think we would lose this pregnancy. The first one was "just a fluke," but out of an abundance of caution, my awesome doctors requested a few blood draws just to make sure my hCG numbers were climbing as they should. Summer break was drawing to a close, so Adam and I squeezed in one last trip, flying to Denver to see my long-time friend, Amy. Although inconvenient, we found a place to draw my blood while visiting. I remember Amy asking me if my doctor really thought this was necessary. After all, her first pregnancy ended in miscarriage followed by two healthy, successful pregnancies. Spending time with her put my mind at ease. I even walked into a maternity store at the mall that weekend and almost bought a cute top for work, but the image of that dang pregnancy test sitting in my medicine chest flashed before me, and I quickly put the shirt back on the rack. I did not want to jinx this one.

As luck would have it, I started violently cramping as we waited to board our flight back to Las Vegas. I remember lying on the cold, hard floor of the airport, curled up on Adam's lap, tears streaming down my face, trying desperately to keep it together so the attendants would allow me to board the plane. Luckily, we had a row to ourselves on our flight home. As soon as we landed, Adam turned around and left on a business trip. With trembling fingers and quivering lips, I phoned my OB to check on my blood work.

Our second pregnancy ended while Adam was in China. Unreachable, just like with the first. This pregnancy was deemed ectopic (otherwise known as a tubal pregnancy) and considered highly dangerous. With my primary doctor out of town, I had the pleasure of dealing with a substitute during this time. I was preparing my middle school English classroom for the new school year when the doctor called to see why I had not made an appointment to terminate the pregnancy, as if this was old hat and I should know what to do. I nervously explained that I was waiting for direction from him because I was not sure what I should do as I had never experienced this before. Substitute Doctor told me that I was going to die if I didn't make a decision right away and that I needed to grow up and stop trifling with my life. Yeah, that happened!

Technically speaking, he was right, even if his delivery was harsh and hurtful. I knew I needed to make a decision quickly or I might lose the window to save my fallopian tube. When an ectopic pregnancy is discovered early enough one can typically terminate through a shot of methotrexate—a drug most commonly used in chemotherapy. It is also used to stop the growth of an early pregnancy that cannot be aborted from the uterus in a typical way. The non-viable fetus is then naturally miscarried.

Once an ectopic pregnancy grows to a certain size, methotrexate is no longer an option. Surgery, with all its possible complications, is then the only alternative. I was in my seventh week of pregnancy, so the clock was ticking, as I would lose my window in the eighth. Telling Adam that I killed our baby was never a conversation I imagined having. I also did not want to jump the gun. What if they were wrong? What if the fetus was just hiding in the uterus? What if this pregnancy would be the magical exception to all other fated ectopics? What if there was a chance that the baby and I could both survive? Even though the intense pain on my right side was enough to confirm the medical diagnosis, I had to be spiritually and emotionally sure!

After a day of researching, praying, and crying, I knew terminating early was the right thing to do. The fetus would eventually terminate itself and likely take my fallopian tube, and possibly me, with it, if left untreated. So I marched myself down to the hospital, went into the chemo clinic, and terminated. Alone! The metho needle was the biggest needle I had ever seen, and I got it straight in the butt. I was asked to lie down for an hour and was then released as if nothing had happened. I left the hospital and went directly to the ice cream section at the grocery store. The procedure was successful and the pregnancy was over, and all I was left with was a couple of pints of Ben and Jerry's Half Baked.

Rationally, I knew how dangerous the risks were, but my heart wanted a baby so badly at the time that my mind actually considered doing nothing. Dumb, but true! I did not want to grieve again so soon. I still felt like my spirit was healing from the first loss, and grieving a double shot of loss seemed really scary. Like, grown-up scary. The blessing in all of this, as there always is one, was the close monitoring by my doctors. They are the reason the ectopic was caught, and I am grateful for their wisdom and caution in my treatment.

The series of early blood draws is what uncovered the tell-tale hCG levels that are associated with ectopic pregnancy. This number is usually in the hundreds, not climbing or declining. The spotting, cramping, and pain would not have been enough for the doctors to go down the ectopic rabbit hole so quickly. Tubal pregnancies are tricky to diagnose early unless you are being monitored.

Thankfully, my very good friend Kelly was also my OB's head nurse. She was amazing and totally made up for the grumpy fill-in doctor that told me I was going to die. Kelly was the one that suspected the ectopic and quickly put me on the doctor's radar. She also helped walk me through the heavy emotions that came with the confirmation. Kelly gave me the information and support I needed to make the very burdensome decision of terminating. I am so grateful for the principle of friendship and the many ways it has blessed my life over the years. Kelly's kindness was one of those blessings— a tender mercy in a hopeless situation. Despite my gratitude for a saved fallopian tube, however, the fact remained that I had just lost two pregnancies in the span of six months.

The Cross of Infertility

After our second miscarriage, a light haze of sadness constantly loomed as I tried daily to reconcile the emptiness that sudden pregnancy loss had brought to me. I was in survival mode at school—my poor students. I was an adequate teacher and did my job. I met deadlines and followed lesson plans, but I was not the fantastic teacher I had been in years past. Having to traipse to work surrounded by children who had not-so-great home lives exacerbated my sadness. I cried every single morning. I cried every single night. And every single day I slept until the last possible minute to get to work on time. I constantly "begged" Adam to let me quit. And this went on for months.

My sweet, anchored husband was more patient than any spouse should ever have to be. He indulged my laziness, never suggesting I was crazy. We both knew that things were not quite normal, because how was infertility normal? There were many times Adam suggested that I talk to someone, but he never pressured me. He was wise enough to trust that I would find my own way to work through my sadness, whatever that meant. As time ticked on and different doctors began running tests, I started to experience twinges of bitterness. Didn't the fertility gods know that I was loudly climbing up the stairs to the doorstep of thirty and I had a large family to create?

I was (secretly) angry. I was angry because everyone around me seemed to keep their babies in their bellies, and I could not. I would like to say that I kept faith, that I was strong and steadfast, but I mostly felt faithless. For a few months, and to my mortal shame, I did not pray much, my scriptures gathered dust, and I avoided friends' children as much as I could without drawing suspicion. I was motivated and successful in the rest of my life, but the grief and emotional turmoil from the pregnancy loss had beaten me down to the point where I started to not privately recognize myself.

As I was driving home one day, lost in thought, a voice whispered (well, actually shouted), **"Rachel, this is to be your trial. Stop feeling sorry for yourself. Let me teach you!"** I pulled the car over, and the thought came again. Whoa! It had crossed my mind that we were running a string of bad luck and I needed to be more faithful. I had figured it was just a matter of patience and faith and time. But no, I had a distinct impression that day that this, infertility, was to be my cross, and it wasn't going away anytime soon. I remember sitting in my car somewhere along Boulder Highway in Las Vegas, cars whizzing by and tears streaming down my face as I cried. I cried for the babies I had lost and the babies I would continue to lose. I cried for the babies I might never have, but mostly I cried over the self-serving pity I had shown myself for too long.

I wanted the world to revolve around me so badly. I wanted a baby. I wanted to be a mom. I wanted to be included in the mom circles I ran in. I wanted to feel competent in that part of my life instead of stymied at every pregnancy turn. But God taught me that day on the side of a highway, in time suspended, that me not having a baby did not equal me being less than. Right then and there I refused to be so! I would no longer dwell on the past, but instead look to the future in faith with an attitude of gratitude in everything I did.

I made a decision in that small moment of clarity: if this was my trial, I would not waste the time spent in the thick of it in pity and bitterness. I would not waste my child-bearing years paralyzed by fear. I chose to let happiness back into my heart, to not be a lame victim who focused solely on the might-have-beens, wishing my life away.

I allowed the Great Teacher to do what He does best, to mold and shape my imperfections into something more. Honored and overwhelmed to be given such a trial to navigate, and knowing I wanted to be a mom, I resolved to do whatever was necessary to get there. At that point, I had no idea what that would actually look like, but I did know that I would be a mom somehow when the timing was right. I also knew that learning to walk the path of infertility with true grace would bless me, my family, and others.

Choosing a Path

With open hearts and minds, Adam and I decided to take my doctor's advice and try a few rounds of Clomid, the go-to fertility drug for most OBs who aren't sure what the problem is. Clomid, that dreaded first line of fertility defense, is not a magic bullet. In fact, it fails more times than it succeeds and royally messes with your body in the process. While enduring rounds of Clomid, Adam and I also started researching fertility clinics and adoption programs. We dug in and searched the vast array of solutions on both fronts. I had no idea what was going to happen, but I knew I had to figure out what my options were because Clomid was a long shot, at best.

We interviewed a couple of fertility doctors but felt like cattle as we were prodded through the clinic's halls, watching dozens of other women waiting their turns. It was so weird! I did not want to go back, but I wanted to be a mom, so I was tempted. At that time, just a few years out of college and newly married, we could not justify spending tens of thousands of dollars on the hope of a maybe baby. It was just too risky for our pragmatic minds.

We also started vetting adoption agencies. China was the obvious adoption option for us considering our work and language ties to both Taiwan and China. However, we were too young and had not been married long enough to qualify for the China program. We then checked out a private domestic program through our church. We went to a couple of meetings, but that too did not feel right. At the time, Adam was not ready to commit to an infant adoption, so we kept looking. Finally, we stumbled across an international agency that had a few different options we would qualify for, so we attended an info webinar they were offering on potential programs.

The options seemed endless, each with possible risks and rewards. It was overwhelming, and I felt like it was tearing me apart. I wanted to throw up most days because my stomach seemed to be in a perpetual state of anxiety. I couldn't be all in on any one decision because I still wasn't sure what was right, which way I should go. The Clomid did not help. It made me feel like I was newly pregnant all the time. The hormones, moodiness, and exhaustion, not to mention the schedule tracking and constant processing of my emotions with Adam made me feel miserable. After three cycles, I could not take any more. I quit Clomid.

The Moment I Knew

Spring 2007

Wow! Where do I go from here? I am frustrated, confused, amazingly disheartened and completely torn. One moment I want a baby—the next I couldn't care less. Most of the time I feel like I shouldn't even try—that we should "just" adopt. I think I am okay with that. In fact, I would be totally okay with it if I knew with certainty that there wasn't a little unborn spirit(s) that needed to come to our family.

It's like, do I do all that I can to "have" a baby and do the adoption thing part time, OR do we focus on adoption and take bio babies as they come (if they come)? I have been trying to give equal time and emotional energy to both, and it is not working. I vacillate too much because I read fertility boards and books and adoption boards and books, and I go over the what-ifs ALL THE TIME!

Being on Clomid makes me emotionally react as if I am pregnant—which means I cry constantly and feel like I have no control. What does it matter, really? If we can't have a baby it is not the end of the world. The most important thing to me is that I am doing God's will, that I can rise up through this trial positively and with grace. I want him to be proud of me—I want him to see the personal growth I so badly strive for in adversity.

So I guess the only thing holding me back is fear of the unknown and the question, "Am I doing God's will by not pursuing further medical treatment?" It looks like it is solely between me and God. I have complete faith that he knows how much I want to please him, and how much I want to be a mom! :)

Just two weeks after writing this journal entry (and over two years from my first miscarriage), my specific prayer was answered.

I was home by myself after work one day. Our nursery, which I had painted a soft, neutral green, housed some boxes of old papers that I needed to go through. I generally avoided this room for obvious reasons, but on that day I went in to try and clean out some paperwork. I was sitting on the ground flipping through old files when I decided to lie down, something I was doing more and more frequently, as fertility hormones had hijacked my body. I remember lying on the carpet looking up at a bookshelf containing a few collected nursery trinkets, when all of the sudden, life went dark, and seemingly out of nowhere, I lost it!

No, really, I seriously lost it. The ugly cry had nothing on this epic meltdown. I remember rocking back and forth in the fetal position, holding a little white lamb that a friend had given me after our first miscarriage. Ten minutes, twenty minutes, thirty minutes went by and I was still crying. I was wailing, sobbing, silently pleading for relief from the compounded grief of lost miscarriages and stolen hopes. I was begging for clarity so I could move through the grief and on to being a parent, somehow. I couldn't stop crying even after my eyes had swollen shut and snot had crusted to my face. I thought for sure the neighbors would hear me and think something awful.

As I was anguished in complete hysteria, something I had never experienced before, I desperately reached out to Adam and asked him to come home. The years of longing had finally caught up with me. I had been secretly drowning for a really long time, literally clawing for solid ground every day, and not managing to grab hold. My mind had been lost to a state of winter where the thick fog of self-doubt clouded the visibility of my future.

Finally, and just as I thought I could not take another sad second of grief and uncertainty, I hit the proverbial bottom, and a flash of light immediately filled the room. It was a distinct and somehow familiar feeling that instantly blanketed me in a soft, yet powerful warmth, working its way from my insides out as it swept from one side of the room to the other and back again. I was completely enveloped. As this molecular moment surged through the room, anxiously rushing to overtake me, my mind was filled with knowledge and my heart was filled with peace. Instantly!

In an instant, my long-time prayer of pleading had been powerfully and unmistakably answered. The things revealed to my mind seemed as though they had resided inside of me forever. My winter of what-ifs quickly resolved into a sweet spring of light and hope. I was left with the confidence and conviction that I previously lacked to move forward on a specific path. I finally knew that adoption, specifically international adoption, for us, would be a blessing. That it was good. That it was right. I no longer needed to feel guilty about choosing that path to parenthood over fertility treatments. I also clearly knew that I would probably never carry a biological baby in this life. I knew that our quest to be parents and to adopt children would bless many lives seen and unseen, not just ours. And in that singular, electrically charged moment, I found myself. I found my purpose, my mission, my life's work. I found motherhood.

Adam came home and wrapped me in his arms. I recounted what had happened and we cried together for a really long time—sad and happy tears. When I told him that I didn't want to take another pill or do one more test or pursue fertility treatments, he smiled and said okay. When I told him I didn't care what our children looked like or where they came from, but that I just wanted to be a mom and that I was certain about moving forward, he began to glow. I can still remember seeing his countenance illuminate goodness and light through the mostly dark room we were seated in. Out of all the adoption options we diligently explored throughout the year prior, we chose right then and there to adopt a sibling group from Colombia. Our prayer was answered, and we knew it was right. We didn't know when or how it would happen, but we knew it would happen. We decided to stop treatments and start the adoption process. Tiny glimmers of hope sat in my heart that night as I dreamed of my future family.

Getting There

The next several months of our lives consisted of both Adam and I quitting our jobs, moving to Utah for Adam's graduate degree, and selling most of our possessions including my car. Needless to say, adoption was on the backburner. We knew how expensive an international adoption was going to be, so we decided to table it until his year-long course was finished. We really wanted to adopt, like right away, but we just couldn't imagine funding both endeavors, being jobless and all.

Most private adoptions are super expensive. The specific program we were looking at was going to run us $30,000 or more. Fertility treatments, IVF in particular, would run us about the same, so either way we were kind of stuck. I knew we would need the boost in income to help fund our future family dreams, so we went for the MBA first, putting ourselves in an adoption holding pattern.

Ironically, by October, only four months after starting Adam's master's program, we couldn't take waiting any longer. How was that for resolve? We had caught the adoption bug, and I was desperately feeling the need to start the process. Our barriers to entry were miraculously coming down. Adam's work had thrown us an unexpected surprise. His company in Las Vegas asked him to stay on during his schooling with the promise that he would continue working for them after he graduated. Details were worked out that became an amazing blessing for us during school, and beyond. In September, a dear loved one offered to gift us some starter money for the adoption fund. I think the exact words were, "You need to do this adoption right now. How much do you need to get started?" As it turned out, all of the obstacles to "we can't do this right now" were mostly gone. By mid-fall, we were ready to turn in our application for Colombia. There were many unknowns, but we decided to just make the money work and pour everything we had into the adoption. It was worth it to us!

Things moved quickly after that. We received a referral for a sibling group of five in November—right before Thanksgiving, in fact. We were so excited—for about three days. We lost that referral the next week. There was some unusual mix-up in the process, and another family had already taken them. We were bummed, but not devastated, which looking back was a sign because when we received our next referral, just ten days later, my heart changed forever. I *knew* we were supposed to take this group. They were exactly what we were meant to do with our lives. At the ages of eight, seven, six, and five, Daniel, Esmeralda, Maria, and Juan came into our lives.

The rest of that school year whizzed by with lightning speed. Adam was busy with school and work, and I was busy with adoption paperwork, keeping our adoption blog updated, and preparing to move back to Las Vegas. The adoption actually ended up coinciding exactly with our year away at school, a nice unexpected surprise. By the time we moved back to Las Vegas in June, we were waiting on travel plans from Colombia. That gave us just enough time to find a place to live, buy a minivan, and prep everything needed for four children to come live with us. You know, no big deal!

And really, it was no big deal. It was everything I had been hoping for, kind of like nesting on steroids. I was surrounded by family and friends that were just as excited about the niños' arrival. Earlier in the spring, Adam's family threw us an adoption shower to end all showers. Instead of registering for baby bottles and diapers, we registered for camping gear and baseball gloves. I think Adam even sneaked a Wii onto the list.

April 16, 2008

Yeah, pretty much cried all day today. Our adoption shower was the most amazing thing that has happened so far on this journey. It was a culmination of so many things for me: the shower I always thought would be for a newborn, a celebration of life with friends and family, and the support and love of so many people in one place at one time. It really was brilliant!

Not only was I overwhelmed by the outpouring of gifts and well-wishes, but also by the genuine support, love, and excitement of so many people. Since it was more of a party for everyone than a girly shower, we were able to celebrate with all of our friends (even the boys). All of our Las Vegas friends were there—staying the whole time and creating a truly joyful experience for us. Adam's dearest friends from work came and showed their amazing support of our decision. Many people from church also gave generously to our little ones. And last but not least, our families were there. My sister Jaimee and her husband even flew down along with my mom.

A huge THANK YOU to Adam's mom, Debbi, and his sisters for putting their hearts, time, and money into the event. The house was decorated in Colombian colors, w/delicious food and a huge cake. One dish was even a Colombian chicken dish that Debbi made—yummo! We know how much work this party was to pull off, and we appreciate it so very much. How blessed are we?

We hope for future opportunities to repay the kindness, generosity, and love that have been shown to us and our children. And it was a total blast. I never knew a shower could be so much fun, seriously!

After the event, my friend Jaime Lynne helped me prepare the kids' backpacks with goodies from the shower. She kept the little packs lined up in her house by the front door for two months. I couldn't bear to take them from Jaime's house, even after we moved back to Las Vegas. If I moved the backpacks, I felt like I would jinx the upcoming trip. I can still picture those pint-sized bags, packed with symbols of family and love, under the front window patiently waiting to travel.

Preparing our new home in Las Vegas was incredible. By the time we were able to move in, we only had about two weeks to unload, unpack from Utah, pack for a month in Colombia, and prepare the children's things. My mom came down and helped me put the house together. Adam spent every night until we left hanging pictures and shelves. My girlfriends spent countless hours helping me sort, organize, and prepare. We sifted through mounds of clothing donations, unwrapped all of the new shower items, packed suitcases for the trip, and wrote an endless number of thank-you cards. Finally, we had two rooms ready and four beds full of welcome-home trinkets. I was fully nested and ready to go. All we needed were the children.

LIFE LESSONS

Blessings Abound
if We Look Up Instead of Down

Over the years, infertility, my trial of faith, has proven to be a blessing a hundred times over in a thousand little ways. Friendships with people who have never heard my voice nor seen my face have emerged. I have formed kinships with beautiful women who each have a mother's heart and who struggle with the same issues as me, women of different religious backgrounds and different geographic locations, but who are bound together as women of faith, women of goodness, and women of action. They have taught me so much about real living, about sticking with something even when it's hard, and about learning to love birth parents even when I want to scream at them for past actions that scarred their children's hearts. I am better because they are in my life. They teach me so much about real love and purposeful living.

Opportunities for increased understanding and increased compassion have blessed me tremendously by choosing to look up. How often do we judge another's status, parenting decision, or path in general? Hearts softened, lessons learned, lives touched, and souls healed have all come to pass through my associations and decisions born from infertility. I am more intentional in my actions toward others and more purposeful in my relationships. This has all come from walking through the Refiner's fire. My family has been blessed through the experiences and compassion of others. My children have found life-long friends with similar life stories. What a blessing that has been to them. And in turn, through those relationships and beyond, we have been able to lift others up along their own topsy-turvy pathways. **God uses those who choose to be used.** It's as simple as that. I have seen this play out time and time again. Exquisite joy can come from deep grief, but we must first choose to be refined, choose to be used, and choose to look up.

Remember the Why

For anything of value, there is always a price to pay. The struggle—the price—is what makes the reward worth it. Experiencing bitter to know the sweet. Feeling sorrow to know the joy. Enduring anguish to know the peace. We all have different motivations for doing what we do. If our *why* isn't rooted in importance, whatever that is for each of us, it is difficult to sustain the needed motivation to keep going. Parenting kids who have been abandoned or have experienced trauma is no different. However much I wanted to be a mom over the years, my personal desire to fill empty arms is not the reason I do what I do. That desire alone could have been filled in much "easier" ways. Rather, it is my children's chance for bright futures that keeps me going. The hope that they can each be healed and live full, beautiful lives is my why.

Every once in awhile, I forget my purpose and I question our family planning decisions. It can be kind of crazy around here. One time we had twelve kids under twelve. Yeah, crazy! On those days and in those moments, I just think about our once empty nursery and I remember. I remember that I would not trade my niños' sweet faces for anything in this world—not ever. They are the reward, the sweet, the joy, and the peace. Every pregnancy loss, every cry for relief, every meltdown and tantrum, every single moment of sadness, it is all worth it! Every day, it is worth it.

CHAPTER TWO

A Family Begins

August 2008

Dear Little Ones,

When Daddy and I woke up on the morning of August 5, 2008, (ten months after filling out our first adoption application) we knew our lives, and yours, would change forever, and we were very excited. Daddy was really nervous. I was surprisingly calm. In fact, I had not been nervous or anxious since we arrived safely in Bogotá. Grandma Penning said that this was the first time she had ever seen your daddy visibly nervous. She was probably right—we do not see that side of him very often because he is so steady and even by nature. I kept teasing him that if he had been emotional and anxious over the past year like I had been that he wouldn't be nervous at all.

We were staying at the Radisson Hotel, and everyone there was so nice and supportive. The girls at the front desk thought we were crazy, but in typical generous Colombian fashion, they thought that despite our craziness, you deserved a home, and they were glad that we were in their country to provide that for you. Everyone was warm and kind.

Finally, the moment came to leave the hotel. This was it; it was time to meet you. We quickly rushed our bags to our new hotel and headed to CRAN (a non-profit foundation that works in conjunction with Colombia's child welfare program to help displaced children) to go over final paperwork and wait anxiously for you. CRAN's head facility (which is a different location than the actual orphanage you lived at—Club Michin) is in Sabu in West Bogotá, right up against the mountains. You were hidden away in one room while we finalized paperwork. Ximena, the founder and director of CRAN was simply wonderful. Her kind, warm eyes showed great concern for your well-being, and she was very grateful that you were going to gain a home and family.

Once we were ready to receive you, Ximena and Maria Cristina (Ximena's assistant) took Grandma out of the room so she could get video of you waiting. When each of you laid eyes on her, we heard "Abuelita, Abuelita!" rocketing out of your mouths and down the stairs. You knew exactly who she was, and it took a room of workers to hold you back. Grandma was actually the first to meet you. When it was finally time to let you come meet us, grandma said you were like a tiny herd of elephants as you stampeded down the hall toward us. As you entered the waiting room, you were so excited, beaming from ear to ear. Each of you couldn't wait to show us your schoolwork and your photo albums that we made for you. You hugged and kissed both Daddy and me. Nikki [Maria], you wanted to sit on my lap. Juan Pablo, you wanted to show Dad every single piece of paper you owned. Esmeralda, you wanted to talk to both of us so much so that you could not decide who to talk to first, and you looked so gorgeous in turquoise that day. Daniel, you stood back that morning, just as excited, letting your brothers and sisters get in on the action first, in true oldest brother fashion. You slowly and eventually brought your photo album over to me, carefully still protected in bubble wrap, with the biggest toothless smile I had ever seen.

After about fifteen minutes with all of you, the psychologist and social worker came back into the room to say their goodbyes and take pictures. It was a sweet moment. When you realized you were leaving for good, however, Nikki began to melt. She curled up in a little ball and wouldn't let go of your beloved psychologist. We were eventually able to pick you all up and carry you out. By the time we hit the courtyard, Nikki was holding Daddy's hand and all was right with the world. We loaded you each into the van, and that was it. We were off, as a family!!!

Settling In

After finding some lunch, our first order of business was to get the children some shoes. We brought plenty of clothes and other necessities from the States, but there was no way for us to prepare for shoes. In fact, as we were walking home from lunch, Nikki started crying because her feet were hurting. Grandma checked her shoes and discovered they were two sizes too small. We then checked the other children and found the same thing! Needless to say, we headed straight to the shoe store instead of back to the guesthouse. Thanks to Grandma's graciousness, each child came out of the Stride Rite store with a new pair of tennis shoes and a new pair of church shoes. More "new things" than they had ever known before. Nikki literally skipped all the way home.

Our first night as a family was spent snuggling up in the same bedroom. The kids ran in and out of the bathroom filling cups of water and dumping them down the sink. Never having unfettered access to running water before, they gleefully turned the faucet on and watched with wonder as the water freely flowed. The children's new, joyful gratitude for this one basic need was the best part of that whole first day, a shadow of things to come in their immediate futures. After wrestling, playing with water, and reading, we squished the two smallest children into bed with us and put the two bigger kids on a mattress at the foot of our bed. In the middle of the night, Juan woke up screaming, "Papi, Papi, don't go away." He was terrified. Adam and I were still running on adrenaline, so despite being exhausted, I don't think we slept at all. We just sat in bed watching them all sleep.

A few days later, we moved into an apartment in Bogotá, which was much more comfortable for us. The guesthouses in Bogotá were well-suited for a couple adopting a baby or one small child, but not for a large family like ours. Having an apartment helped us feel more like a family and helped us keep our new children contained, as they were curious about *everything*.

Moving to an apartment meant grocery shopping. We decided to take everyone on this adventure so the kids could help pick out some of their favorite foods. The market nearest our apartment was comparable to a medium-sized grocery store in the US, nothing supersized by any means. When we walked up to the store, however, you would have thought we entered Disneyland. Not in their wildest dreams did our children ever conjure such a place. To start, the automatic doors totally blew their minds. In and out, giggling with wonder, they ran through the doors several times. Once inside the grocery store, we rocked their little worlds again. Rows of fully stocked shelves and fresh food aplenty caught our children motionless as their eyes scanned this new phenomenon. We raced carts down the aisles choosing foods that looked interesting to each of them. Picking out cereal was the *highlight*, even trumping the ice cream section. Their favorite cereal ended up being Zucaritas (Frosted Flakes). I am sure they didn't even know what was inside the box or how to eat it, but Tony the Tiger won their hearts. Zucaritas it was. On a side note, boxed cereal in Bogotá was extremely expensive, which we expected. It was so pricey though that we had my dad bring a whole suitcase full when he came the next week. I was never so happy to see a yellow box of Cheerios in my life.

As we approached the checkout lane, the kids became visibly agitated. I thought it was because they did not want to leave the glorious rows of cookies and candies. I assured them we would come back, but that did not seem to calm them. As Grandma Penning and I started loading food onto the conveyor belt, the two youngest, Nikki and Juan, started crying. Ezzy and Danny were quiet but clearly upset. When I asked them what was wrong, they too started to cry. Then it hit me! They thought we were putting the food back. Duh, why had I not considered that angle? Adam showed them what the checkout line was for and that we had to pay for the food that we wanted to take with us. Once they saw food going into bags and then back into the cart, they understood and were able to calm down. Phew, major meltdowns in public averted. And major lesson learned.

We spent the next couple of weeks reinforcing that there will always be enough food. Fortunately, in Colombia, our children had access to enough food in their institution. This is not the case in many countries. We were prepared to help the children with food hoarding and related issues but hoped that they would not have to deal with it long term.

Fortunately, our niños did not end up having many struggles with food. They did have to adjust to not being on a strict food schedule like they were at the orphanage. The children also had to learn to give themselves permission to eat seconds and to make choices when choosing a variety of foods—that was a little overwhelming for them at first. We kept to a pretty strict food routine since that is what they were used to. After a couple of weeks, we slowly adjusted to a more natural food rhythm that fit our family better.

Convincing the three older children to stop giving Juan their food during mealtime was no easy task in the beginning. They wanted to make sure he had enough, and our little garbage can was more than happy to oblige. Even when his belly was completely bulging, he would still beg for more. After about a week of routine and redirecting, the older children naturally connected that food was readily accessible and stopped being so generous with their portions. Juan's gluttonous feasts did not last as long as he hoped, I think.

Goodbye Honeymoon Phase

After a week or so of settling into the apartment and into family life, the children's behaviors started to deteriorate, as expected. Prior to the adoption, we prepared as much as possible for this inevitable letdown, but let's be honest, there is no amount of training that is equal to real-life experience. Our "honeymoon phase" was abruptly over. It literally took three adults to manage the first two weeks— monitoring, soothing, tag-teaming, keeping up in the kitchen, even the simplest of daily tasks. We lovingly refer to that period as "the Dark Days." And we self-medicated each night with chocolate cake and Diet Coke!

On one of the very darkest of those days, I almost thought I had made a mistake. I was new, and it was pretty bad. Juan was in his bedroom for hours raging back and forth, biting, pinching, and spitting as he thundered. Imagine a small animal in captivity for the first time. I am sure this is how little Juan felt as he transitioned from orphanage life to family life. He was kicking and clawing at the door, screaming for his sister, and shouting obscenities at me (words that no small child should ever know at five years old). As that was going on in one room with Adam, I was with Nikki in my bathroom sitting on the floor in front of the door so she wouldn't bolt out of the apartment. She screamed and screamed and screamed because she wanted to leave our family. And when she wasn't screaming she was trying to punch me in the face. Before long, Adam had to leave Juan because Daniel started raging in the front room. He was angry because he wanted to watch cartoons instead of obeying our regularly scheduled quiet time. Seriously?!? Of course he picked this moment in time to have his first epic tantrum, going toe-to-toe with his dad. At least Ezzy had fallen asleep during the breakdowns. I am not sure how we would have managed all four!

After about an hour of this madness, Adam managed to calm Danny and then came back to rescue me—first checking on Juan, who had since fallen asleep on his mattress. Nikki was safely curled up under the sink sulking. I was curled up on my bed, also sulking, exhausted by it all. Adam looked at me lovingly. Then, lying down next to me he gingerly wrapped me in his strong, comfortable arms, and we softly sobbed together.

The entire first week in that tiny Bogotá apartment found me crying myself to sleep. You name it, I felt it: panic, anger, sadness, exhaustion. Adam and I dealt with communication barriers, spoken and unspoken. We spent hours upon hours modeling a proper family structure, setting expectations and consequences. We also found ourselves rapidly teaching life skills such as how to use a fork, how to use the bathroom, how to touch only one button when using the elevator. And the list went on. We were inundated with a steady stream of seemingly basic tasks that our children didn't know how to handle. They had never been to school, not a real one, anyway. They had never had a play date. They had never prayed, went school shopping, or attended a birthday party. They had never been sung to, read to, or comforted by a loved one, not that they could remember. Our sweet niños came to us with one outfit and the shoes on their feet. That was it. What they lacked in wardrobe and physical possessions, however, was far and away eclipsed by what they lacked in social skills and emotional intelligence.

Most of us grow up in a family unit inherently learning daily tasks and social rules from infancy, the repetitive, mundane things that we simply take for granted. Starting from ground zero with these already walking, talking, expressive children was emotionally taxing and physically exhausting. During those first few weeks of parenting, every single ounce of my body hurt.

Aside from crying for the obvious reasons, lack of sleep, heart-breaking moments of terror, adjustments in my marriage, and really adjustments of every kind, I was also crying for a million and one silent reasons. I wished we had found the children sooner. I wished we could have cared for more children left behind in the orphanage. I wished their first experience in childhood had been the very best this world had to offer. I wished their parents had made different choices. I wished they could still be in their native land, speaking their native tongue, enjoying their first family.

On the flip side, I wished I had birthed each of them and that I didn't have to share space in their hearts. I still wished I could have a baby, and that made me feel guilty. I wished for a friend that would understand exactly what I was experiencing. You name it, I wished for it. Nothing about adoption or fostering is fair—to us, our children, or their birth families.

No matter my wishes, this was our reality. We signed up for the good days and the bad. We signed up to help these children become brothers and sisters, not just random kids birthed by the same person. And these were my children now, my responsibility. "Mami" and "Papi" suddenly emerged as my two favorite Spanish words. However bad the tantrums were or how escalated the screaming and the raging became, we were all in this together, no matter what. And very slowly, each day of adjusting became a little less dark, a little more normal, a little calmer, a little more like family!

Empty Arms no Longer

Bogotá was the perfect place to stay for the month while we waited for *sentencia* (adoption finalization). Although we were dealing with emotional trauma and adjustments, most of our days were spent having fun. There were tons of things to see and do. We visited a children's museum. We went swimming. We made several trips to a pizza place which housed a monster slide. We took a cable car up the mountain, Monserrate, which dominated the city with spectacular views. We took a day trip to Panaca Sabana, which was kind of like a glorified petting zoo with pig races and other random events. The kids loved it, especially milking the cows and riding the ponies. We employed an English tutor to come a few times a week to help give the children a little schooling, also. But mostly, our days were filled with puzzles, movies, walks, and coloring. The everyday, normal stuff families do together.

Wedged in between our apartment building and the river was a lovely little park with a long walking path attached. We spent hours at that delightful patch of green, flying, or rather chasing kites. There was not much wind, of course, so getting the kites to fly was an obvious challenge, but that did not seem to matter to our kite chasers. Rain or shine, one could find our kids running with their kites.

Daniel and Ezzy would start sprinting down the concrete path trying to get them to take flight. The kites trailed behind bobbing and skipping across the ground. Not far behind, Nikki and Juan chased after them. For hours upon hours, up and down the path, with giggles and delight, they chased those silly little kites. And wouldn't you know they willed those flimsy pieces of plastic into the air. They kept running, keeping the kites delicately gliding along just above their heads. Until, eventually, the junior kite chasers would catch up to their big brother and sister, yanking the kites down to the earth. Each child would fall to the ground laughing with pure, unfettered joy. Over and over, they played this game. Their legs were free to run, their hearts were free to feel, and their minds were free to dream. And dream they did.

The amazing thing about a kite is that the more forceful the resistance pushed upon it, the higher it flies, the better it performs, and the more stable it becomes while in flight. Our kite chasers had much resistance in their early lives. From abandonment and missing relationships to extreme poverty and lack of education, they experienced deep resistance. But just as with a kite, resistance of all kinds—the trials, pressures, and struggles of life—is also what helps the chaser to fly.

During the adjustment phase with our children, and before the adoption was finalized, we were called into the office of a government official for a meeting. (In the States, the equivalent would be a lawyer representing the Department of Family Services.) We thought we were going there to sign paperwork, etc., which we did end up doing. The actual point to this gathering, however, was to give us the chance to send all the children or even just two of them back, just in case we had changed our minds. In astonishment, when we were asked if we wanted to return the children, Adam and I looked at each other and instantly answered in unison, "NO!"

Even though I was shocked by the question, not expecting it at all, I believe it is good and right to give people, both the adoptive parents and the children if they are old enough, the option before moving forward permanently. There is wisdom in this approach, especially when the decision involves moving children out of their home country, losing their citizenship, losing their first language, etc. It is a thousand times better than disrupting after the fact.

On the other hand, I could not believe I was being asked the question. And they were serious; I really had a get-out-of-jail-free card if I wanted one. Despite the anger, the sadness, and the tears, in just a few short weeks, these four little strangers had become my children in every way. There was no way I was going to let go of them.

Even in the very darkest hours, I did not want to go back to my previously empty arms. And more importantly, I did not want them to go back to the cold, dark halls of the orphanage. There was no future for them if they stayed there. I was their future. And I knew we would be equal to the task by and through grace, not because of our capabilities alone. Christ's grace was sufficient then and continues to be today. Grace blankets us in the hard times. It nourishes us in times of spiritual famine. It increases our gratitude in times of bounty. Grace literally makes all the difference. It is the difference. The true brilliance of grace is that it is sufficient and free for all. Utilizing God's grace is how Adam and I beat the dark days so many years ago, and it is how we continue to push through in the darker parenting moments of today.

The Orphanage

One particularly gloomy afternoon, just after lunch, our taxi pulled up near our children's orphanage. Dark clouds loomed overhead. Heavy rain had just fallen and was threatening to fall again. The air was chilly, the streets eerily quiet. There was no traffic to note, no dogs barking, and no typical city-like sounds anywhere. I felt instantly sick as I stepped out of the cab and onto the wet, dirty sidewalk. We had left our children at the apartment with my parents while Adam and I trekked across town to tour the facility where the kids had spent the previous three years of their early lives. There was no way I was taking them with us, as they might think we were going to leave them there. Walking down the street as slowly as possible, I methodically traced every step with my eyes, taking mental notes of the buildings, the street signs, the smells. I lingered on the sidewalk across the street from the mish-mash of complexes that constituted the orphanage. I did not want to go inside. I knew it would change me, and I wasn't ready, but it had to be done.

As we entered the first house, Daniel's house, there were about 30 eight and nine year olds, all boys, hanging out of the barred windows completely unsupervised, in the middle of the day—instead of being at school. Once inside, we could not find an adult, anywhere. It dawned on me that this was a daily reality at this orphanage. It was normal to them. The television was blaring as the sounds ricocheted off the cold, concrete walls and benches in the common area. There was nothing warm or cozy about this place. There was no carpet, no heating unit, no fire or stove. There was no warmth to speak of. The play yard consisted of more concrete enclosed behind the kitchen with limited access to light. It was literally concrete against concrete with no play set and no grass to speak of. It was the antithesis of the little park near our apartment where they were free to chase their kites and run free.

Each child had one pillow, one blanket, and two changes of clothes. Clean water is at a premium in Bogotá and is prohibitively expensive; all orphanage residents had water rationed out to them for teeth brushing, drinking, showers, etc. Actually, because of the expense of water, children were only allowed cold showers. Yes, cold, as in not lukewarm, but instead whatever-came-out-of-the-pipes cold!

There was one chaperone for every thirty children, and that chaperone left at night to go home. The children slept alone, unsupervised, with no one to sing or read to them, no one to tuck them in, no one to quiet bad dreams or anxiousness, and no one to fill the tiny holes of abandonment pricking their little hearts.

Just as the facility had no physical heat source, the children within the facility were starved for emotional warmth. As we visited the different houses, this became more and more apparent. The children clamored for attention, fighting to be first in line to get a pencil, a sticker, and sweet treats we had brought. Yes, we were a novelty, but it was more than that. I had been a novelty when I taught English in Taiwan and when I spent a summer in Zambia. I knew what that felt like. This was different! The children did not just gawk at this blond-haired, green-eyed, tall white spectacle, which is the usual response. Instead, they wanted to be noticed by us, hoping they might have the same chance that we were giving to Daniel, Ezzy, Nikki, and Juan. They wanted us to take them. We spent about an hour talking with the children, handing out goodies, visiting our kids' rooms and beds, meeting their friends and their caretakers. And all the while, behind my smile, my heart was breaking into a thousand tiny pieces.

I could not take them all, but I wanted to. The children in this orphanage, as with all government-funded orphanages in Colombia, were not stolen from their parents. They were not sold to the highest bidder. They were not in the orphanage due to corruption or human trafficking. Most of them were there as unintended consequences of the ongoing civil war and accompanying drug trade that has ravaged the country of Colombia for decades. Extreme poverty is pervasive due to these issues, and extended family members, by and large, are unable to care for the thousands of children affected.

This was exactly the case with our kiddos. Their grandmother and aunt tried to care for them, but even with assistance from the government, it was not enough to sustain the family's basic needs. Poverty and lack of resources made it impossible for them to succeed. The government tried everything they could to help keep our four kids together. In the end, they ended up in a welfare institution for three years where they were eventually set to be split into two groups and freed for adoption to the international community. When we stepped in and said we would take all four, they were literally one referral away from being split up, perhaps even living in two different countries.

A War on Adoption

I wish desperately that poverty did not exist, anywhere, ever! I wish that war didn't tear families apart, that drugs and alcohol and other addictions never turned children into beggars on the street. But they do, even in the richest, most self-actualized countries in the world. Poverty does exist. War does exist, and always will. People will always have a choice to engage in addictive and corrosive behaviors. And there will always be evil people trying to gain from this. There is most definitely corruption in the adoption world. It is sickening and wrong, but it is not an excuse to thwart adoptions of children who are in true need of care and of a family. Human trafficking and baby snatching are not what line orphanage halls with children. Death, war, drugs, and incarceration do that all on their own.

Colombia is one of the only places where the international adoption treaty formed at The Hague (guidelines for inter-country adoption, including protection against child trafficking, corrupt adoption practices, etc.) has actually worked positively. Colombia's child welfare agency, ICBF, does everything it can to place its children in Colombia, as they should! They do have a foster care system, although it is not robust enough to encompass all children in need yet. The Colombian people are naturally warm and caring, and children are typically treated much better than in a lot of other countries. We witnessed this during our adoption, not only with the child welfare workers but also with people in the general public.

The working relationship Colombia has with the international adoption community is also well-functioning and stable. It runs a child-focused system that tries to keep siblings together and to place legally-free children as soon as possible, whether in or out of its own country. So while Colombia is building community awareness platforms and driving in-country adoption campaigns, they are also not holding children back in orphanages and foster care while they try to "fix" the system. They promote harder-to-place and older children through hosting programs; they give incentives for keeping sibling groups together. They work really hard to take care of their orphaned children. It is not a perfect system, but it is better than in most countries.

There is a better way than institutionalizing children. In the meantime, though, as countries try to build foster communities, promote adoption, and help families who are destitute and addicted, what do we do with the children that languish in these institutions? Do we just leave them there because we feel that it should be different? Do we just throw our hands up and politically spin a minority of corruption cases worldwide to stop ourselves and others from helping the larger majority? That doesn't make any sense, at all, but people still believe this stuff, and worse yet, say it on forums, in Facebook groups, and other places where only portions of correct information are being plastered and debated.

Conflicting views on adoption are many. The news spews stories of parents sending kids on airplanes back to other countries, birth parents legally maneuvering for children post-adoption, adoptees who were lied to, adoptive parents who were lied to, birth parents who were lied to. And the list goes on.

There are adoption groups out there, some of which I belong to, that have members who strongly condemn adoptive parents for internationally adopting, stating that we are most likely part of a child trafficking ring or corrupt adoption agency scam. Some have even said that we have no business adopting at all. They believe that education and resources designed to keep struggling families together are *all* we should focus on. Really?!? Have these people ever been to an orphanage in Mexico, or Eastern Europe, or anywhere, for that matter? We as content consumers must educate ourselves, for ourselves, not just relying on shocking headlines on Facebook or in our Twitter feed. This work is too important to politicize.

As churches, communities, and governments diligently try to mobilize a better way for struggling families worldwide, my efforts focus on the realities of right now: lines of children laid out on mattresses, literally head to toe for naptime, some crying, some quiet, some actually wasting away. As I remember the orphanages and the poverty and war-torn families I encountered in Colombia, I don't much care to wait on slow-moving governmental systems. I care about the children who are hungry for hope and light and goodness right now. They do not deserve to sit in limbo for years while policies are made and programs are considered.

There is so much goodness in this world. And some of my most favorite models of goodness, my children, came from a Colombian orphanage. I am grateful for an adoption agency and the Colombian government, who worked cooperatively to bring our family together. It is my hope that none of us let fear or misinformation stop us from moving forward, spreading light, and sharing goodness, not the least of which is helping a child obtain the best parts of this world by gaining a family through adoption.

Hugging my children after our orphanage tour was more surreal than when we first met them. I was so glad they were safe with us, never to return to that place. I hugged them and snuggled them the rest of the day. However, I was also sad and guilt-ridden over the children who were left behind. Like my niños, some of the children had been there for years and would likely never be adopted. Too many kids, not enough homes. The best thing I could do was focus on the children I had just adopted, giving them opportunities to thrive, and also hoping to maybe return one day and adopt just one more.

Touring the orphanage did change me, but in all the right ways. My trip would not have been complete without visiting. Although it was difficult to go, I gained valuable insight into my children that

I would need as I helped them transition into their new lives.

Helping Hands

After the orphanage tour, Adam and my parents stayed in-country as long as they could, but they each had to get back to work soon after. I could not manage the children and adoption appointments all alone, so my sister sent her husband, Brian, who spoke Spanish. And one of my very best friends, Jena, also flew in to help me through the end of our stay. Left and right, friends and family dropped everything to support our adoption effort; this was just one more example. Brian left during the height of his company's very short busy season, and Jena left her one-year-old daughter to help us through this crazy adventure.

Uncle Brian stayed for several days and took my parents' spot, cooking, cleaning, and errand running. He kept the house moving while Jena helped me with the children. He even made piña colada smoothies for the kids one night. They thought he was the coolest uncle ever, especially when he wore an apron and helped them operate the blender! In fact, Daniel wanted to be just like Tio Brian, so he coined himself "Batman Brian." I have no idea how Batman came into it, probably because he thought Batman was cool like Brian. Regardless, it was adorable and the nickname stuck for a really long time.

Jena stayed with me to the end: shopping, packing, checking out of the apartment, navigating the consulate, and of course traveling home. She endured the tantrums and enjoyed the laughter. She supported me through the frustrations, the screams, and the smiles. And she never said a word about how I should do things differently. She just let me do what needed to be done, even when it was hard to watch. Jena was let inside the rawest part of an orphanage adoption, and she loved my children regardless. Experiences like what we shared together in Bogotá are very rare in friendship. Everyone needs a friend like Jena. I am blessed enough to have several!

Finally, after all of the adoption boxes were checked, and with traveling papers ready, it was time to leave. We said goodbye to Colombia and made preparations to head back to Las Vegas. The desert. The heat. Together. And just like that, we were off.

LIFE LESSONS

Adoption Is Not for Everyone

Adoption is not for everyone, it just isn't, especially and specifically adoptions that are not domestic, infant adoptions. I used to believe when well-wishers would say to me, "I could never do that," they really actually could if they chose to. I believed they were just being kind and trying to compliment my efforts. Adoption does not require perfection or super-human abilities. Average, ordinary people like me succeed at it all the time. But let's face it, not everyone is equipped to take on three, four, five children with language barriers and past trauma. Not everyone has a similarly committed partner, the financial means, or the pragmatic disposition it takes to move through the hairy moments and difficult questions that come as a part of this journey. The month we spent in Colombia took two very in-tune, very devoted, very patient partners, as well as one full-time grandma, an uncle, and an awesome friend to keep the house operational. If I had a different personality, or if I had a different husband, or if I was not 100 percent committed to this forever, I would have quickly found my way back to the comfortable emptiness of my desert home.

The thing about adoption is that it takes true commitment and hard work well before becoming a parent: mounds of paperwork, uncertain time frames, potential fundraising, tons of research and parenting classes, reconciling loss when you are not chosen or you are rejected from a program based on religion, family size, etc. And this is just a quick summary of pre-adoption hurdles and tasks.

Although adoption is not for everyone and the barriers to entry seem insurmountable at times, the one and only thing adoption truly *requires* post-entry is a loving, committed heart. I am not talking about "Saviorism" (that is a topic for another book).

What I am talking about is true love, true compassion, and true commitment. If you have the heart and you have the commitment, you can succeed with the right training and preparation. If you are willing to do the research, put in the time, access the resources, and open your heart and home no matter how the child may receive or perceive you immediately and in the future, then you *should* consider adoption. Adoption *needs* people like you.

Discipline Is Organized Love

Out of all the things Adam and I have done right, discipline is what we have done best. Discipline is so much more than bossing and task-mastering. Don't get me wrong, we run a tight ship and expect a lot. We are firm. We are organized. We do what we say and we say what we mean, and we are very consistent with all of it. But none of the work we put into teaching boundaries, self-mastery, and rule-keeping would mean anything without the motivation of love to back it all up. The key that unlocks any successful parenting paradigm is LOVE.

My own personal increase of love was found in a dark, dreary orphanage on a nameless street in the heart of Bogotá. It changed me. The compassion I felt for my children as we walked away from that place is unlike anything I have ever experienced. As I toured the facility, memorizing glimpses of my children's former life, God not only expanded my worldview but also expanded my capacity to love.

A decade later, I still feel that surge of visceral compassion when I think back to that day. I can see it, smell it, and feel it. The toddlers lined up in rows napping, the unchaperoned eight-year-olds roaming aimlessly, pleading for us to take them with us; the lines of tables being set for the next meal, the sweet mountain rain misting the streets. I remember it all. And my compassion continues to increase, which not only strengthens me in the hard times but also allows me to parent really hard behaviors with love as the constant motivator.

It is so hard to parent and train and tutor the right way. It is really difficult, complicated work. Visiting the orphanage made me resolute to lead with love. I wanted all of our children to grow into our family and love it, and to also feel the love within it. I wanted them to know that everything we did, and continue to do for them, was born out of love. Without the love part, discipline is simply, and only, punitive. We all know how effective that is. Deep, unconditional love has saved me many times when correcting behaviors and handing out consequences. It has saved me from losing my temper on countless occasions, it has saved me from saying hurtful things that I knew I would regret later, and it has saved me from many moments of irrationality, frustration, and anger.

Remembering to discipline from a place of deep-rooted love allows grace to work in my life, as well as my children's lives. When I ask myself, "What would the Savior do in this situation?" Or "How can I draw grace down from Heaven right now?" I am able to re-center myself, my motives, and my actions. There is no magic bullet, no tricky or hidden secret to parenting. It is simply organizing our love in effective ways.

Love and genuine compassion are what truly move the disciplinary needle. Nothing else will do. Other remedies such as fear or coercion may temporarily stop a behavior, but without an immediate increase in unfeigned love after the correction, those tactics are short-lived, and the capacity for the person you are disciplining to change is significantly stifled. Discipline requires gentleness, persuasion, and temperance, which must be present in all we do with our children if we desire true, heart-driven change. There really is no other successful way. Haunting cries from the orphanage remind me daily to speak Love, always!

CHAPTER THREE

Coming Home

N ever have I seen a kid as happy as Daniel was when our plane took off from Bogotá. He couldn't stop staring out the window, and he had the biggest, brightest grin. His little legs kicked faster and faster, trying to keep up with the plane's acceleration. As the plane started down the runway, rapidly gaining speed, all four children shouted, *"muy, muy rapido"* completely unscripted and in unison, which made our entire section of the plane laugh out loud. I will never forget that first take-off. Jena and I still laugh about it today. The niños were super ready to finally go to their new home. Their excitement was palpable. I am sure they were anxious about the unknown, but mostly they were just eager for the adventure, and to be reunited with their new daddy.

The kids were awesome travelers. Each of them handled plane changes and customs like they were born to be our children. What was even better than watching the kids have fun on the plane and navigate their first airport experience, though, was watching them wrap their arms around Adam when we landed stateside. Seeing him standing outside LAX next to our newly-purchased minivan hugging our children as they rushed to greet him was totally and completely surreal. Finally, we were home!

One of my dearest friends, Marisa, traveled down to LA from Ventura to meet the kids and to drop off individual traveling care packages. She sewed them each a travel blanket (which they all still have today), she packed them each a bag of snacks, crayons, and trinkets, and she made a CD of children's songs in Spanish. Man, did we wear that CD out over the next year. I still have "Soy una Pizza" tucked away in my memory under "music I want to forget, but not really."

The five-hour drive home was blissful, which I realize is oxymoronic when talking about traveling with children, but it really was. I kept turning around to see beautiful, smiling children in our car. Miraculously, every time I turned around, they were still there. It was the best feeling in the world, even when we stopped on the side of the road in the sweltering heat to help little Nikki go to the bathroom because she drank her entire bottle of water in a matter of minutes (free water was still a new

concept). I felt nothing but pure elation. The feelings I felt the entire trip home were indescribable.
No fear, no trepidation, no wondering if it was right,
just awesomeness. Maybe it was jet lag, or maybe it
was adrenaline, probably a combination of the two.
Regardless, our car was full of potential futures and
love. The best part was that it was simply full!

Juan and Nikki thought their car seats were the
coolest things ever. Danny and Ezzy were annoyed
that they didn't get to ride in one. Yep, they both
pouted. Over a car seat. None of them had ever seen
a car seat before, let alone sat in one. We stopped at
Great-Grandma and Great-Grandpa's house in Vic-
torville for root beer floats. The kids went nuts over
Grandpa's grand piano and his organ. And, well,
root beer floats bridge all international barriers. It
was the perfect pit stop.

The rest of the drive found the children mostly
silent as they took in the changing scenery. Bogotá
is located in a high plateau of the Northern Andes,
which is over eight thousand feet above sea level. It
is green, lush, rainy, and temperate—the complete
opposite of our children's soon-to-be home. Needless to say, they were awestruck by the stark desert
landscape, mountains of rock and vast open spaces.
No translation necessary; it was different. And they
were soaking it all in.

We arrived on the outskirts of Las Vegas after
dark, the children asleep. As we woke them up,
they noticed all of the dazzling Vegas lights and

started chanting "Las Vegas McCracken, Las Vegas McCracken." Danny's sweet, husky voice with his Spanish accent was to die for. Family and friends welcomed us with banners, flowers, a stocked pantry and fridge, family-time baskets, and hugs all around. It was a most memorable night. I knew there were a lot of hard, taxing days ahead of me, so I chose to enjoy the moment for what it was, a sweet homecoming, just the way I pictured it.

A Bundle of Firsts

Non-stop visitors graced our home the very first week. Despite the experts' advice on bonding, attachment, and over-stimulation, we felt that the love and support of our friends and family would only help the children feel more secure, as they were pretty happy and outgoing kids by nature. Our entire support system was phenomenal in directing the children back to Adam and me as the authority figures. No one tried to take on the nurturer or disciplinary roles. Also, living life as usual, right out of the gate, gave us the chance to teach the children about hugging and touching people who are not mom and dad. It was slow to come, but they began to form healthy attachments with others as they practiced obeying boundaries in family and social situations.

I know this is not the way for everyone. There are many right ways to do things, especially to parent. This way worked for us, and it worked wonderfully. The first month home we went swimming, camping, out to eat, over to friends' and family's homes, shopping, to the movies, and hiking. Instead of shaping our lives around these new little creatures, we chose to insert them into our existing adventurous life, and they loved it. They loved the activity. They loved the burgeoning affection they felt by our circle of influence. They loved the opportunities. They loved school. Amidst the emotional struggles and language barriers, the kids were finding their happy.

After a couple of months home, Ezzy came out of the shower one day very perplexed. Her face was squished up as she looked in the mirror, and I could tell she was thinking. I asked her what was wrong. In broken English, she said, "Mami, I was in the shower and I looked down and my feet were white (pointing to my skin), but my legs were brown." She was laughing with delight at this new phenomenon. When I realized that she had never had a tan line before, I couldn't stop laughing too.

My guess is that she thought her skin color might be changing to match mine. We talked for a few minutes about what a tan line is and how the sun makes our skin darker. She thought it was the weirdest, coolest thing ever. She spent the next few minutes checking out her bathing suit tan lines in the mirror. Neither of my girls had ever owned a swimsuit, let alone been out in the sun long enough to notice their skin change colors. Can you imagine? AMAZING. At seven years old she began a love affair with swimwear, which has continued into her teens.

Summer turned to fall, and the holidays were soon upon us: county fairs, trick-or-treating, pumpkin carving, caramel apples, roasting turkeys, and baking pies. Our children drank their first fall in like a long, warm sip of soothing cider. They weren't freaked out by new traditions. Instead, they were totally in love with the newness of family and the delight of the changing seasons.

Celebrating the niños' first Christmas was nothing short of magical. Christmas 2008 was a celebration of true miracles both seen and unseen, an answer to silent yearnings. For years, Adam and I had celebrated Christmas together—yet alone! There were many moments during those child-less Christmases that I cried tears of sadness and longing. Behind every holiday smile and happy celebration, there were private moments of deep, emotional pain.

After three years in an orphanage, and despite their congenial dispositions, our new little niños were still scared, awkward, and unsure about a lot of new things. They had never seen a dishwasher or clothes dryer before, never actually been to a real school or to church. As for Christmas, at the ages of five, six, seven, and eight our Colombian kiddos had never trimmed a tree or sung a Christmas carol. They had never experienced a holiday family meal or heard the nativity story. Imagine, they had never given or received a Christmas gift—ever! My children, like so many other sweet orphans in this world, had never partaken of the thousand little Christmas traditions we hold dear in our homes and in our hearts. Twinkling lights. Sleigh bells in the snow. Wise men bearing gifts. Santa Claus and the North Pole. You name it, our kids had never even dreamt of such things, so you can imagine how magical that first McCracken Christmas was to them and to us.

My parents flew in on Christmas Day with suitcases full of presents, mounds of sweets, and well-wishes from Washington. Santa Claus showed up at Adam's parents' door with giant candy canes and gifts aplenty. And of course, that Christmas was when they first heard the nativity story, understanding line upon line what the very first Christmas and Jesus' birth was all about. Our niños slept under the tree that year and were delighted with joy at each and every turn. I remember quietly sneaking down the stairs and watching their bright, happy, sleeping smiles. The magical balm of Christmas with its perpetual rays of hope was silently working its magic on our kids' hearts. I could physically see their souls healing through the magic of Christmas that year. The magic of giving. The magic of family. The magic of tradition and love. And above all, the magic of Christ's atonement—his greatest gift. Ironically, as I solely focused on the kids' happiness that first Christmas together, parts of my own heart were healed. Watching the delight on my children's faces helped soothe my long-time heartache.

I am so thankful for that very first silent night. The one that brought another family together; where a newborn baby was born, whose life was consecrated to bless and heal the entire human race. Thousands of years later, I recognize that first Christmas's hope in my Colombian children—in Danny's smile, in Ezzy's goodness, in Nikki's sweetness, and in Juan's forgiving spirit. And that is truly magical!

Turning Firsts to Memories

Our lives were full of many more firsts that year: a new language, playing in the ocean, Yahtzee, fruit pizza, homemade waffles, swimming pools, backyard barbeques, backpacking, Scouts, dance class, learning to ride a bike, shopping at Costco and Target, and everything in between. It was all new to our niños. That year of firsts delighted our home with wonder and laughter. A year of memories and of miracles!

I tried to document every first that I noticed in an effort to make up a little for the undocumented firsts of their lives before us. Everyone experiences firsts throughout their entire lives, but for our kids, the remembrance will never be as complete as it could be. When the day comes that each of my children individually start exploring his or her past, mourning the gaps in their early lives, I hope they will be somewhat comforted by the firsts that I was able to record—knowing that from the time I was charged with their care, the things they experienced and learned and discovered mattered to me.

I long to know about their past lives, and I can only imagine where their personal wonderings will one day take each of them. Will they search? Will they investigate? Will they move back to Colombia? Will they find what they are looking for? What were their toddler years like? Who watched them take their first steps? When did each of their first steps occur? Who was there in those beginning weeks to see them smile and coo for the first time, and who changed their diapers and perhaps rocked them to sleep? I would give anything to know where all of the nicks and scars on the boys' bodies came from. Whenever I traced their skin that first year, I thought of that. I wondered who the first person was to truly bond with each child. When did they learn to talk, to smile, to brush their teeth? Were they bathed regularly, were they soothed when hurting? But for now, and maybe forever, all I have are the firsts that we created. I pray that it is enough for my children and that if it is not, they will each find their own "enough" someday.

Because of the children's ages when we brought them home, I felt like I was watching and experiencing firsts in fast-forward. This is where purposeful parenting pays out in large dividends. When we brought the kids home we were very cognizant that we had less time to teach, train, prepare, and enjoy them. Being tuned into that knowledge shaped our early parenting decisions.

Together, we spent as much time as possible doing things that mattered. For us, that meant family, faith-building, and fun adventures. It meant protecting family dinners and weekly family time. It meant turning off the TV, putting down the computer, and plugging into each other. It meant purposefully deciding to participate in only the "best" activities. Through intentionality and dedication, the niños experienced explosive growth in the areas of bonding, language, and social skills. Their futures were made even brighter by the education they were receiving in and out of school. It is truly remarkable what faith, focus, and love can accomplish when put to the test. The growth and healing occurring within our home stood as a living witness to that end. What we do as parents matters.

Looking Beyond

Becoming a mom meant I had my own personal year of firsts as well. Soothing hearts into the night, shuttling carpools, and creating dinner menus were just a few line items from my list of mom firsts. My most significant first, however, came with an unexpected pregnancy and subsequent miscarriage.

February 2009

Finally, I had "that" moment. For months I have waited and wondered when it would actually come. *This morning, as I awoke from a very vivid dream, it did. It **finally hit me that I am actually a mother of four children**. And not just any four children, but four little Colombian strangers who I would never have known, let alone have the opportunity to mother if it wasn't for our faith and hope in adoption. I no longer feel like just a caretaker who loves them deeply; instead, I feel like THEIR MOM!*

Every day I realize just how fantastic my reality really is. I did not create my children one, or even two, at a time. I went from zero to four quite literally overnight. Why am I not overwhelmed? I should be overwhelmed. One awesome August morning, at the age of thirty-two, I woke up, packed my bags, drove to a lush hillside on the outskirts of Bogotá, and instantly became a mom. How does this even happen?!? It's the coolest way to become a mom, I think. It's not the easiest, but definitely the coolest.

And maybe these recent answers and reflections on adoption are tender mercies from heaven to help me cope with the latest miscarriage. This miscarriage was weird, to say the least. I mean, it was unexpected, short-lived, and just weird all the way around. Part of me is too busy doing mom stuff to think about it much. And the other part of me doesn't want to go back to the familiarity of functional darkness. And yet, the thought of that familiar place is so very tantaliz-

ing. It's kinda like a drug. You fight so hard to be healthy, happy, and functional. But one misstep, one weak moment of self-pity can take you right back to zero. Luckily, I am becoming a pro at healthy grieving. I believe the niños have helped with that.

I am so grateful that my experiences have given me not only perspective but also wisdom. The niños demand all of me, all of the time, and that is a job worth doing well. We still want a baby. The kids want us to have a baby. I SUPER want one, but only for my own fulfillment, not because I need it to feel like a real mom. That probably makes no sense. We don't crave a baby. We don't pine for a baby. We don't hate people with rear-facing car seats. I mean, come on. There is so much more to living. And I love that I now feel that deep down in the seat of my soul.

As for fertility, I guess this particular miscarriage takes us back to the proverbial drawing board. We were just getting to the point where we thought we might start deliberately trying, so I guess the timing couldn't be any more perfect. Do we try? Do we call it quits? Do we do more testing? Do we go back on Clomid? Do we...? I have a consult with Dr. S on Tuesday—we'll see how it goes. Decisions, decisions.

Obviously, the miscarriage itself wasn't a first, but how I felt after it was. I remember telling Adam when we came home from the doctor, "Just give me a few days of peanut M&Ms, ice cream, and Diet Coke, and I'll be good." And it worked. Of course, I was a little sad at losing the prospect of a baby, but I wasn't devastated. My deliciously lovable children were my new coping mechanism, my new drug!

It wasn't just the distraction that they created for me, but also the hugs and the loves and the sense of belonging that they offered me. It was everything. We certainly still wanted to have a baby, but we were not willing to sacrifice our time and emotions that would take us from the niños. It was so soon after the adoption; it just didn't feel right. So after consulting with my OB, we tabled any discussion of fertility treatments and focused on our existing family. They continued to soothe my broken heart in matchless ways that first year home. First miscarriage post-adoption, check! Although I considered the aftermath a success, it did leave me a little unsettled and left me wondering what was in store for our family in the future.

LIFE LESSONS

Make Your Life Happen

We have taught a "No Victims Allowed" mindset from the moment we became a family. Our mantra has been "Don't let life happen to you. Make your life happen." Our family motto is Decisions Determine Destiny. This is a core belief that we teach in our home. We teach that past experiences are just that, they are the past; but also that our futures are built on the lessons learned from the past. We do not try to shove those memories down or pretend they do not exist. We did not bury our children's former lives on the streets of Bogotá. Rather, we use the lessons learned from enduring those experiences to make our lives better and to bless others. What we do right now matters. That's it. Right now! What will we do with our today?

How do we teach young children and teenagers to be doers instead of victims when their worldview is so narrow, when thinking past their own tomorrows is nearly impossible? One word: service. We have modeled this foolproof method from the beginning. My husband's heart is wrapped up in service and his family. Our kids totally hit the dad jackpot when they came into our lives. From the time we brought our children home, Adam took them every time he helped someone move—even when the kids were tiny and couldn't do much. Every time someone's lawn needed raking, wood needed stacking, or a car needed fixing, Adam would take the kids, leading by example. McCrackens serve, even when it is inconvenient, because guess what, it is always inconvenient. What better way to teach children that the world does not revolve around them or us, that no matter how bad of a day we might be having there is someone else who is suffering more? Selfless service teaches that being a person of action, more concerned about others, can snap us out of any selfish funk.

The beautiful part of this method is that it requires family work and parental example; no one is off the hook, and everyone benefits. We serve together. We serve with happy hearts. We serve because it makes us better and because it is the right thing to do. Service unlocks the path toward true charity—the pure love of Christ. When we possess charity, this most priceless Christ-like attribute, our selfish attitudes fade, our pride is replaced with humility, and our spirits are filled with gratitude. This is when we see miracles happen. When we swallow ourselves up in helping others, troubles and pains that seemed so overwhelming before suddenly become less important, and sometimes even become irrelevant. I have seen this happen time and time again in my children's lives, and my own. I have seen with my own eyes the miracle of God's grace at work, healing our children's hearts and making them whole as they focus on others.

Teaching children of trauma to erase or hide their past is to rob them of opportunities to strengthen themselves and others. Instead, we must train them to use that trauma and abandonment, the good and the bad of their childhood, to help bless others. And at the very least, we must help them to not remain a prisoner of it.

My children are certainly not perfect. And they make tons of mistakes. They have each been unkind, selfish, and downright dumb at times. Just like me. Just like their dad. Just like everyone. However, they have overcome enormous odds. The deck was stacked highly against each one of them early on, which makes their progress quite remarkable. They are quick to forgive. They are quick to show compassion. They are quick to be friendly. I attribute their incredible emotional headway to the curative powers of faith, family, and service, all under the umbrella of God's amazing grace.

CHAPTER FOUR

Molecular Moments

W e used to have a large family portrait that hung in our living room in our first home. I loved it so much. It was a beautiful reminder to me of the struggles and decisions that led us down the path of adoption. Every time I walked by it, I smiled. When we first brought the children home from Colombia I could not envision that family picture any other way. If a baby came along, great! Otherwise, it was perfect—just the six of us.

In fact, as time went on I would stand and stare at the portrait trying to imagine more children, mostly for my husband's sake. We had always wanted a really big family, but the ups and downs of adopting and the subsequent realities of bonding and parenting left little in my mothering gas tank. Adam, on the other hand, was ready to adopt again from the moment we got home. He's that kind of guy.

Every time I thought about another adoption, though, my palms would sweat, my heart would race, and my knees would buckle. I worried about disrupting the family groove we had created. It is a lot of work to whip a little family into shape. I also worried that the next adoption would not go as smoothly, that I would not be able to handle new behaviors, or that I might not love the new kids as much as the old ones. As with fertility so many times before, I once again felt like the broken one. I mean, what was wrong with me? Adam was good to go. I wanted to be more like him, more trusting, less over-thinking. Deep down, I did want more children, but I was not sure my heart could handle another adoption. So I decided to use our family portrait as my readiness gauge. If I ever felt differently about adding to the family when viewing the portrait, which I was quite sure I wouldn't, being broken and all, then I would allow Adam to use his heart-melting magic on me!

In September 2009, exactly one year after arriving home from Colombia, I accompanied Adam to London on a business trip. Adding to our family was a hot topic on the airplane, as it had been for several months. Gratefully, I had lots of time to ponder while away in the English countryside. One day while Adam was off working, I sat at our room's picture window people-watching on the golf course. I had the window open so I could breathe in fully the cool, damp breeze, a stark contrast to the stale, summer heat of the desert.

While thinking of all things Jane Austen, I caught sight of a little family golfing. The dad was practicing his swing while the mom and pre-teen daughter were chattering on in the background. They were having a good time just being around each other. What caught my eye was how much the mom seemed to be enjoying her daughter. As I was thinking about that, the wind picked up and it started to rain. The mom quickly and tenderly took the daughter's hood, pulling it up over her head, smoothing the daughter's wind-tossed hair around her face, all without missing a beat in their conversation. She hugged her tight for a moment, and then went back to her previous stance as if she had done nothing.

It was one moment in time. And as quickly as it came to that family, it left. But for me, it lingered. It was the moment I had been waiting for. That specific and solitary moment in time picked itself up and made its way through the swirling wind, through my open window, and into my open heart. It stamped itself forever there. In that one supercharged moment, molecular if you will, I knew I was ready. I knew that when I saw my family portrait again, I would feel peace about adding to our family. And that is exactly what happened. I can't explain how

I knew, how my heart changed; it just did! In one single moment, it changed.

Seemingly meaningless mommy moments happen a hundred times a day for those of us who mom. We mom without thinking about it, it is just what we do. Even if we are a little slow at getting there, nurturing is in our nature. If moments are the molecules that make up our eternity, then these countless mommy moments are paramount to our existence. They not only impact our own forever, but also the forevers of our children. Hopefully, my personal mommy moments breathe joy, peace, and consistency into my own children's eternities. I decided in England that I wanted to give more potential forevers to more children.

The miraculous thing about my experience in the countryside was that it led our hearts to somewhere I never anticipated. It was the one place off limits in my mind when thinking of creating a family. On the plane ride home from London, I agreed to attend a foster care orientation class with my husband just to "check it out." We had considered another international adoption, but the price tag was very high and we were still dealing with language barriers. Fertility treatments still seemed too risky, as there was no guarantee and our finances were still recovering from Colombia. Foster care was our only immediate option. I began to prepare my heart for the roller coaster of emotions I was about to ride.

Our end goal was to adopt, but we were prepared to foster, doing good along the way.

My only previous exposure to foster care was one super "weird" family I semi-knew growing up. Although I was committed to trying, I had hesitations, biases, and many limiting beliefs—none of which were really about the children inside of the system, but rather the adults that care for them. My one early childhood encounter built foster care up in my mind as the big, bad place that crazy people go to earn money. I had so many questions and uncertainties. I worried about how others would see me. Our little McFamily already didn't fit into most family molds. How would those we encounter treat us if we had foster kids too? Yes, I absolutely worried about appearance and perception. And what about having to give kids back? That seemed like enough to do me in after losing so many pregnancies. Yep, I naively worried about that too. I was ready to take a chance, but I was not sure if my heart could handle another break. Many selfish thoughts played through my mind. I know thousands of others feel, and have felt, the same way, for better or worse. Nevertheless, in true McCracken style, I committed to trying.

Ready or Not

The foster parent training classes in Las Vegas were surprisingly good. I attribute this to our trainer, Lani. She was the best. Lani was real, open, and committed. She helped frame the realities of foster care in a positive light and helped make our transition into foster care as smooth and comfortable as possible. There was certainly no pretense; we were well prepared and given honest instruction, but she also provided rich opportunities for us to catch the hope-filled vision of reunification, mentoring, and serving the hearts of children who suffer the most. In Las Vegas, the trainer also licensed new foster families when we went through classes. It is not done this way in every state, city, or jurisdiction.

Some states compartmentalize and/or contract out their education and licensing departments. We loved the Clark County model because new foster parents were able to develop a real relationship with their trainer over a period of months beginning with training classes and continuing on all the way through home study and home visits. This provided less anxiety for the potential foster family, at least it did for us. It also provided continuity and consistency through the process. By the time we received our license, Lani knew us, our children, our capabilities, and our hearts. The best part of our experience was that Lani became an advocate for us. We were friends at that point, and she truly wanted the best for our family. And all these years later, she is a friend still!

Fostering Gets Real

September 10, 2010

We had yet to receive any placement phone calls since being licensed for foster care last week. And then yesterday, all of a sudden, I fielded five inquiries! Apparently, there has been a problem with the call system, and it was finally updated yesterday. I received one email from an adoption recruiter, one phone call about a foster placement, two respite phone calls, and one emergency shelter call late last night.

*The placement we are most interested in is an adoption placement of three siblings ages three, five, and six—girl, boy, boy—Latino, mostly Spanish speaking. Sound familiar? All we know is that our family profile has been **potentially chosen**. What does this mean? Um, not really quite sure. We did fill out an Adoption Interview form during training, but I think it is a pre-screening sheet of sorts, so they do not have to read the entire home study, in case we do not match up.*

I am not really sure what the procedures and timelines look like. We have not been able to talk to the recruiter on the phone yet. But I figure I should document the whole shebang, in case it comes to fruition. And even if it does not, I want our next set of children to have as much back-story as possible. And I figure there are others out there toying with the idea of foster care, or adoption through the state. So once again, here we go!

I am thinking right now about how much we are needed. If on the day that my profile is finally released in the system I get FIVE calls, this service we are about to provide is unfortunately sorely needed. Some (including me) say, "Just because you can, doesn't mean you should." Others (including me) say, "If not us, then who? If not now, then when? If not here, then where?" Both lines of thinking are relevant. It is in the balancing of both that we can do the most good. We can't "save" them all. But we can parent and train and love as many as we feel inspired to help.

I do not want to be a good mom. I want to be a great mom. And I want to be a great mom to as many children as Father in Heaven directs me to. And there's the rub: following inspiration's guidance so that I am never in over my head, but also constantly challenging how much I think I can do, because it is in those exact moments that my compassion grows, thereby blessing the lives of everyone around us.

I still have so many fears, and I know that I will waver at some point. Yes, I am totally crazy. This is well-established. And yet, I feel like the overarching fear and dread I have felt the past nine months is being lifted from me as I plunge forward into the unknown. It is being replaced with an overwhelming sense of peace. It is difficult to explain in words, but I can feel my heart changing again, much like before when we first decided to travel the adoption road. And we all know how much that adoption has blessed my life.

I have decided to stop kicking against those pesky little pricks and just go with it. It is during these times that I find myself learning the most, growing the most, and giving the most.

Per our foster adoption worker's suggestion, we held off on any placements while we waited to see if we were a match for the three siblings. If we took another placement in the interim, the state would likely not move children around and we would miss this potential adoption opportunity. We waited about a month when I finally got the call. At first I hesitated to answer because I thought it was a placement worker on the other end, and I did not have the heart to keep saying no.

Suddenly, I realized it was a different extension and thought it could possibly be our adoption recruiter. The room immediately started spinning and I started to panic. Was I ready? Was I really going through with this? What if we were not chosen? What was I thinking? I already had four children. Life was good. Did I really want to be a mom again?

Fear paralyzed me, temporarily. I sat by the window at Jaime's house, the same window where my first four children's backpacks sat just two years before, watching the phone ring. Jaime looked at me like, "Hey, weirdo, are you going to answer?" It seemed to ring thirty times before I somehow managed the courage to will my faltering finger to press the talk button. I couldn't breathe or speak. Luckily, the adoption recruiter did. We were chosen!

The children were ours if we wanted them. What? Was this really happening? A legally-free sibling group, ages six and under? No fostering first? No significant delays? And by the way, "Could you come and meet them next week?" she said. "If you think it's a good match, we can start to transition fairly immediately," she said. "Hmm, let me think about it," as if I needed to actually think about it. I called Adam with the awesome news. He was ridiculously excited and supportive, as usual. I had that guy way back at "siblings."

This situation was more serendipitous than any of us realized at the time. Our adoption worker, Stacey, was finally free to share with me the details of the kiddos' case and how we came to be on her list. It turns out she had talked to Lani, our trainer/licensing worker, on the very day our license became active. These two wonderful women, who work in completely separate departments, happened to pass each other at a training class when Stacey mentioned an adoption placement she had. As soon as

Lani heard that it was a younger Latino sibling set, she thought of us and gave our name to Stacey. Stars aligned, the adoption team confirmed our match, and the kids were ours!

Growing by Three

We started foster care classes in January of 2010. By September we were licensed. And on October 31—our all-time favorite Halloween—we brought the Littles home permanently. It was an amazing first week. I can still remember Annie's cute chubby cheeks, sweet dimples, and beautiful long hair. Brian was so shy and timid, yet brave and ready to take a chance on another family. Joseph just loved everything about his new life. The brothers, the Legos, the daddy adventures, he loved it all. Joseph, Brian, and Adriana were everything we imagined when we said yes to their placement. In fact, they were much more than that. Joseph's good-natured spirit, Brian's creativeness, Annie's beaming smile and raspy little voice, it was like I had drawn a winning lottery ticket three times over. God was smiling on our family for some reason. We were so grateful that we had kept our hearts open and taken a chance on foster care.

To shoot a little dose of reality into this situation, everything was not peaches and roses. Making no mistake, there were some major issues with these three little gems. Some of the behaviors we dealt with straight out of the gate were food hoarding, running away, nonverbal communication, and trauma-based anger. We, of course, had an adjustment period, as well as many months and years of correcting behaviors and assisting in emotional healing, especially for Brian. He has given me permission to share part of his story so that someone else might benefit. (Yep, my kids are pretty great!)

We Have a Runner

Brian, age five going on six at the time, was significantly traumatized by the events of his past and subsequent abandonment when we received him. Not only was he behind in language, gross motor skills, and educational developments, but he was also diagnosed as severely emotionally disturbed when he came into care. That sounds super scary on paper, right? I know it scared me. It was my first encounter with a real diagnosis.

Brian was completely non-verbal when we received him. He would curl up in a little ball in the back of his kinder classroom, scared of everything and everyone. Running water and loud noises frightened him to death. Emotionally, feelings of unworthiness and inadequacy were two hurdles this little guy needed to overcome. In the beginning, Brian would cry or tantrum at the slightest hint of being in trouble or getting something wrong. Being scolded or corrected at home and at school was very difficult for him. You might be asking, "Okay, but what did that actually look like?" Brian was very sensitive to touch and loud noises. For example, he never wanted to take a shower. I mean, he *hated* showers, to the point of screaming and running out of the bathroom.

For us, the problem wasn't that he didn't like showers, but that he couldn't articulate why. We wanted to help him but didn't know how. He did not mind baths or the swimming pools or flushing the toilet, it was just the running water of the shower that freaked him out. After a couple of months, Brian opened up to me about it when I was bathing him. He didn't like the feel of the water pounding on his skin because it reminded him of scary things at his first home. This is the same reason he would flinch and start screeching like a baby pterodactyl when someone would try to touch him. He would hug us at bedtime, but that was on his terms and part of a routine. Other than that, he rarely liked being touched.

Our Littles' biological father had been deported after Annie was born. Around the time our adoption was finalized, our social worker happened to be retiring and was clearing out her files. She gifted us an entire file folder of notes and pictures she had kept on the family from the beginning. Gold mine! Through this treasure trove of information, we realized that the biological father had been arrested for domestic violence, and subsequently deported. The light bulbs started exploding in my head! The scary stuff that Brian talked about became crystal clear. Whether he had been directly abused or had watched his mother be hurt, we finally understood what the shower kept triggering for him. Pouring that on top of the abandonment and his natural tendency to withdraw, our little guy was pretty broken for a little while.

Brian was also prone to running away, not far and not for long, but prone nonetheless. Mostly he would scurry under his bed or down our street and back again. One time, when Brian was about seven years old, we had a particularly frightening moment. It was about two years after he came to our home. We were at church in Las Vegas in the middle of July. To say it was scorching hot outside would be an understatement. I do not remember why he was having a meltdown, but I remember having the feeling that it was going to be a doozy. About halfway through church, I tagged Adam out from Brian duty so he could go fulfill a church assignment. When I came into the situation, I thought Brian was calm enough that we could walk the halls together. Yeah, I was wrong. As soon as I let go of him, he bolted. He didn't just bolt down the hall or to the bathroom. He bolted out the door, down the sidewalk, and down the street. I would normally not chase him because it would usually escalate the situation, but this time we were not at home and I knew he wasn't going to stop. So I ran, first in high heels and then in my bare feet on the boiling hot desert sidewalk. I had to keep running. I couldn't stop. There were many busy streets ahead.

Brian ran so far that he ran out of the neighborhood and was about to hit a very fast and furious intersection. There was no way I was going to catch him. There was a point when I thought I was going to lose him. Panic started swelling in my chest, and it was getting hard to breathe as I ran. Out of nowhere, a car swooped in front of Brian and stopped. The man inside ran around the back of the car to cut him off. That small diversion gave me just enough time to catch up and grab him before he could slip away again. The man helped me wrestle Brian into the car and drove us to back to the chapel.

We were only one street away from the main intersection when this angel man appeared. The soles of my feet had been burned off. I had no feeling in them and I was shaking. It was 115 degrees and yet I was chilled to the bone. I knew shock was setting in. The angel man who came out of nowhere just smiled and said, "We've all been there, Mom." That's all he said. I don't know his name. I never saw him at church again. I don't know anything about him except that he saved my son's life.

As Adam delivered Brian and me home, Brian quickly understood he had crossed a line. Hysterical, and in shock from the heat, I was crying, Brian was crying, and Adam was crying. All three of us were a hot, emotional mess, to say the least. The ironic part of the story is that once I asked Brian why he ran like that, he responded, "Mom, I thought I was running home. I just wanted to go home."

Um, okay, didn't see that one coming. Needless to say, neither of us could be the least bit angry with him. Frustrated and scared, absolutely, but not angry. Our home was his safe place, and that is where he was trying to get to. After that experience, Brian began making giant strides emotionally and behaviorally.

Several years later, Brian is much better at standing up to the negative feelings he sometimes experiences. He is mostly able to take corrections without melting down, able to keep composure when others are picking at him, and able to articulate his feelings when explaining why he is upset. These are monumental skills that this super pre-teen has acquired. Brian still screeches once in awhile when one of his older brothers won't stop teasing him, but mostly he manages it very well, usually messing with them right back.

Today, Brian is smart, kind, compassionate, and creative. He dreams of playing in the NFL, works hard on the lacrosse field, and excels in school. Brian is an example of what can be. The reality of his "scary diagnosis" is that he just needed someone to persistently and consistently be there for him, someone to hold him accountable and sometimes to simply hold him. Brian still runs from time to time. Once he ran to the back of our property, falling asleep where we could not see him. And most recently, while hiking and rappelling, he ran out of frustration and embarrassment. All in all, however, our kind and witty boy is happy and thriving.

Annie and Joseph had fewer issues, but there were still things we needed to work on. Like Brian, Joseph was also diagnosed as Severely Emotionally Disturbed, but his nature was much more docile than Brian's. Joseph was very slow to anger and could let most things roll off his back. Needless to say, he dealt with his past in very different ways. Most notably, Jo Jo (Joseph) would sleepwalk at the foster home and gorge on food, mostly bread, in the middle of the night.

When we first brought the kids home, literally the very first day, an entire dozen cupcakes went missing. Seriously, where could they have gone? Into Joseph's belly is where. We have caught him diving through the trash for food, mostly sweets. We have witnessed the aftermath of him eating an entire giant bowl of Halloween candy in one hour. Not pretty! We have even caught him opening and eating packets of dry cake mix. Not just any cake mix, but the kind that goes in an Easy-Bake Oven. Yes, he did that!

Food hoarding is real, I can testify that it is legitimate. And Joseph hadn't even been institutionalized. Food hoarding is certainly not exclusive to orphanages, but it is more likely to occur in places where food was scarce and needed to be rationed for extended periods of time. Jo Jo always had plenty of food at his first home and at the foster home before us. For Jo, this was his way of coping with grief, his way of processing the loss of his family and all he knew before us. He came into care between the ages of four and five. He has been with us for over seven years now, and we are just coming into a place where he can control his hoarding impulses. It is so much better now, but sometimes it still takes a little redirection and focus on his part.

Annie, well she was just pure sunshine. She was three and a half when we received her. She certainly had her toddler stinker moments and had to learn about being in a family, but because of her age and bright disposition, it took no time at all for her to fully integrate. We bonded the moment we hugged each other. Annie was very easy to love. In fact, until she was about seven years old, she still believed that I birthed her. It was obvious that I did not, and we talked about it all the time, but there was no talking her out of her own belief system for several years. Annie brought the kind of light into our home that only pint-sized little girls can bring. She was pure joy!

Managing the Tribe

All in all, going from four to seven was not that big of a deal. Seriously, what is another three when you already have four? The Littles complemented our niños in all the right ways. We fell fast for each of their personalities, food hoarding and all! I adjusted much faster than I thought possible with seven children. Going from zero to four was much more difficult. Even if you factor out the orphanage mentality, language barriers, and culture shock, our first adoption was still more of an adjustment because I had only myself to worry about for years and years before that. With the first adoption, I wasn't a mom, and then poof, I was, in an instant.

By the time we were ready for a second adoption, experience had grown me into a more confident and prepared mother. The three Littles fell into a robust family culture of love, structure, and security that we had cultivated throughout the previous two and a half years. Since this culture now existed, the new additions slipped right in.

The niños were great at modeling expectations, which was *huge*! Chore lists, bedtime routines, family dinner, and appropriate displays of affection were all in place and running smoothly. This made dealing with the initial trauma and grief of the three new children so much easier. Even though I had more children to physically care for, I also had more emotional and spiritual reserves than the first time around.

Considering we now had seven children, we were surprisingly free. When our children were very young, my friend Jessica used to joke that we were the most mobile parents of seven she knew. Okay, she didn't know *that* many parents of seven children, but to her point, we refused to let the number of children stop us from doing the things we loved. Weekly date nights, girls' weekends, Daddy camping and backpacking trips, and spontaneous road trips to Washington were McCracken family mainstays.

Our kiddos became amazing travelers. I do not think we did anything special per se to make them that way. We just said from the beginning that Mc-Crackens travel. It's what we do. And the kids kind of just followed. Heck, our family was started by traveling the world to find each other. A decade later, I find my kids getting itchy feet, just like me, if a few months have gone by without going on some kind of road trip. Our family size has never stopped us from doing, seeing, participating, and exploring. We squish together on floors in hotels rooms, squish together on floors at friends' houses, and squish together in the car with all our stuff. It's the Mc-Cracken way, and honestly, it's half the adventure.

Our growing family was also blessed by our af-ter-school nanny/tutor/closet organizer/right hand in all things, Emily. With so many small children, I knew I would need some extra help, and Emily was the perfect fit. She started babysitting for us at age fifteen, and by sixteen years old, Emily became our on-retainer babysitter, growing to love my kids almost as much as Adam and I. Seriously! And when we were able to make the adoption final with Joseph, Brian, and Annie, Emily was there at the courthouse right beside us. She was a blessing to my children and also to me. Having Emily around allowed me to attend all of my kids' events, practices, and non-kid-friendly obligations. My divided time became less so by having a helper. Paying to have Emily around three days a week after school was a budgetary sacrifice that paid out huge dividends to our family.

Emily continues to be a stalwart supporter of my children. They look up to her and all she has accomplished in her twenties. She is invested in their lives, but also, they are invested in hers. As much as Emily has given to my family, we have given value back to her as well.

Emily learned valuable lessons from our large family. She learned how important it is for kids to have structure, how good it is for them. My kids taught her that every person is unique and that different children have different needs; she learned how to be in tune with that. Babysitting my seven very small children (ten and under at the time) also helped Emily learn to embrace chaos, that a little bit of family mayhem now and again is good for the soul. She also learned that sometimes you just have to sit on your child! Luckily, she was never afraid to use that secret weapon, even once the boys outgrew her in size. Positive role models like Emily abound in our family, our friendship circle, and our church community. We all need the village, but in turn, the village needs us just as much!

Future Whisperings

We can let life happen to us, or we can make our life happen. Certainly, my time was divided by the children we added, but my love was multiplied even more. I had heard this theory before, but as I cared for seven small children, I watched it unfold in my own life. Love was not meant to be divided. We make the room in our hearts and homes, and God fills it up with the love and goodness required to pull off his purposes and miracles.

Seven became the perfect number of kids to me. My heart and my hands were fuller than I ever imagined. Having a baby would have still been icing on the cake though. I stilled longed for a baby, but I was also so happy with raising my kids. Seven was a great number, divine even! I thought I was done, finally. And then I had a dream!

I experienced the kind of dream that when you wake up from it, palms sweating, heart racing, mind swirling, you wish you were back in it instead of awake. I dreamt there were two more brown-haired, brown-eyed little ones out there. Somewhere. And that they may have siblings who were afraid of being left behind. As I was driving the next day, with unusual rain drenching the streets of Las Vegas and pounding on my car at the stoplight, I had the same exact dream flash before my waking eyes. At that point, I got the picture. I knew the dream was meant as a message and not some conjuring of my messed-up subconscious. I tabled the dream because I knew it was for later, preparing me, but I kept myself open to future whisperings.

LIFE LESSONS

It Is Not the Size of Your Family, but the Size of Your Heart

Most people have surprisingly strong opinions about family size. Many people in adoption groups, and in general, have said horrible things about large families. Such things include how all parents of big families don't raise their children, but rather make the older children raise the younger ones. How it is just an orphanage with more food or that the kids would be better off staying in an institution. People actually say this stuff, and more disturbingly believe it. I asked my children to define our large family in one word and one word only. Their responses, in no particular order, were "awesome," "fun," "amazing," "interesting," "helpful," "unstoppable," and "adventurous."

This is not everyone's experience with large families. Some are quite chaotic, a mess if you will. But I know lots of smaller families that are a mess too. I have several friends who parent large families and they are the best, most capable, most loving people I know. And I do not mean perfect, because what family or child or parent is perfect? I have personally spent time in the sheriff's office with one child, time with the sheriff in my home with another child, a couple of children have been in and out of counseling, and a couple of children chose to experience "running away" when they were younger. We have even had a rock thrown through a window during one of our children's lowest moments a few years ago, hence the counseling. Yep, not perfect. Not even close. I am super checked-in and I am a purposefully present parent. And yet, life still happens!

The thing is, adopted or not, families aren't perfect. Although I am disappointed at times with my children's choices, I have learned that it is 100 percent not a reflection on my parenting, or me. And sometimes that really sucks, because, like all parents, I sometimes wish I had the power to stop or correct the imperfection, stop the pain and suffering that wrong decisions bring, both to my children and to those whom they have wronged. But that is not my job or my purpose.

My job is to lovingly help them feel the weight of their *own* mistakes so they take responsibility, eventually wanting to correct their own mess-ups and improve. I help them recognize the need for a change in their own hearts so they can choose to live better lives for themselves.

Our only purpose as parents should be to teach, train, and tell the truth. It is not to coerce or manipulate or create a false existence that makes us feel better, or look better to others. That is such a waste of precious time. Stuff happens. Kids do stupid. Adults do stupid. Some of our choices in life are certainly more public than others, but we are all really the same—trying to raise our kids to be productive, healthy, and happy. Small or large, family units sometimes struggle. We were made to struggle; it is the only way to grow. Whether we birthed a child with a certain disability or we knowingly chose to bring a child with a difficult behavior into our home, struggles exist in every unit just the same. It is not about the size of a family, but rather the intentionality behind the parenting.

Whether we have one child or twelve, are we engaged? Are we carving out moments that matter? Are we creating family traditions and culture? What matters most as parents is what we are doing with our family right now. It's about not giving up. Ever! How are we helping our children make their own lives matter? What purpose are we breathing into their lives through our examples and mentoring? Do we expect miracles or expect darkness? Do we spend more time dwelling or doing? Big family or not, I recommit every day to choose to see light, to expect miracles, and to work purposefully to help my children feel the light and see the miracles that abound all around.

Henry

After the adoption of our three foster kiddos we took a year or so off from foster care and focused on building and strengthening relationships within our family. In early 2012, we renewed our license thinking we would adopt one more sibling group and then be done. The first placement we received was a sibling group of two: Henry and Grace. They were ten and twenty months respectively, and so super cute. The children were part of an emergency removal and in need of immediate placement. We picked them up late at night from the receiving facility, not knowing what we would find. This was our very first time picking up a "cold call."

As soon as my eyes locked with baby Henry's, we were both instantly, irrefutably bonded. He reached out to me, clung to my neck, and refused to let go for the next several months. Grace was a sweet little girl that got along well with the other children. She especially bonded to our little Annie at the time. They were inseparable and played all day, every day together. This was a blessing to Grace because she was much more bonded to her mother than Henry was. She missed her mom terribly and had a difficult time after visits. Annie's companionship made the readjustments a little easier for Grace.

Henry was the new baby gem of our family. He was at the best age for discovery, learning to walk, talk, eat big kid food, and stack blocks. You know, all of the things we sit around watching babies do for hours. He loved to swim, eat rocks, play outside, and wrestle with the boys. Man, that little guy could eat. He loved pickles. He also loved to bite our toes. Well, actually, he just loved to bite my toes. He thought it was hilarious and so did everyone else, except for me, of course.

My favorite thing about Henry, however, was his sweet need to be mothered. He would cuddle with me for hours always wanting to be right beside me. I had never parented the instinctual need of an infant before. It was very powerful. And I was so grateful, not only for the experience, but also to fill the mother role for Henry as his mom worked her case plan.

There was certainly a chance we would get to adopt them, and that was made very clear by the investigating worker who met with us first. However, after meeting with Grace and Henry's mom, and becoming mentors to her, we knew it was unlikely. She was focused on changing her life and reunifying. Foster parent veterans know how rare this is. Not only did she say she wanted the kids back, but she also actually changed her life to try to get them back. She started testing clean and never missed a check; she got a job and went to all of the classes that were court ordered. Mom *never* missed a visitation. She kept her promise to stay away from the person who injured Henry (the incident that started the investigation). She kept her promises to us, all of them.

We helped Mom put on Henry's first birthday, and eventually, toward the end of our role as their foster parents, we hosted Grace's second birthday at our home inviting all of Mom's family and friends over to celebrate. Mom also asked Adam if he would be Henry's godfather. He was honored. We loved Mom and her children.

Things weren't perfect, of course. There was a reason the children were in care. Mom had a lot of work to do to get them back, but she was trying, and making great progress. We never stood in Mom's way, and we did everything we could to support her and her children. We knew Henry and Grace would eventually go home, but we were so excited to get to be a part of their lives forever, eventually taking over aunt and uncle status. That was the plan anyway.

Then came the DNA swab that changed everything. Through a series of messy, unfortunate events, we were required to drop Henry off at his birth father's one day, out of the blue, never to parent or see him again. The caseworker had *us* deliver him. We were so new to fostering that we did not realize we even had a choice not to or that this was an odd request.

This was *the* moment foster parents fear the most. It was *the* experience that keeps so many good, amazing people from giving their hearts to foster care. Birth Dad had known about Henry since before he was born but had no interest in parenting, not even after the children were in care. Once his extended family learned the children weren't with Mom, they switched from complacent to angry, pushing Dad to take Henry. The family was relentless, badgering the caseworker so much that she caved and made decisions in the interest of the checked-out birth father, instead of Henry, to appease Dad's family.

Henry did not go back to his birth mom, a woman who had actually worked her plan diligently so she could be reunified with her children. Henry did not get to stay with us where he felt safe, loved, and secure. Henry did not get to stay with his sister. No, Henry was sent to another stranger who happened to share his DNA, who was a kid himself, who didn't want Henry, and who had crazy issues of his own with no idea how to parent. There was no transition, no visitation, no discussion. Henry was just gone!

To make things worse, we were not allowed any further contact with Henry because birth Dad was worried we were going to kidnap him, which underscored the weirdness of the situation. We not only had to abruptly sever ties with Henry, but also deliver him to the very people that thought we were going to supposedly kidnap him. This insanity made the loss of Henry that much harder to swallow. It was wrong on every level. It not only threw us and our children into a state of mourning, but also Henry's mom and her family, as well as sweet Grace, who was now dealing with a second traumatic loss in the space of six months. To top it off, Adam and I had to fly to my grandfather's funeral the same day we lost Henry, leaving our children to initially grieve without us.

Grace was able to stay with us for several more weeks as she transitioned back to her mom full-time. During those weeks she had an even more difficult time when leaving her mom after visits. Grace saw Henry periodically during this transition time, but she could not understand where he had gone in between those times. Years later, she is still with her mom, growing happily. And we have no contact with baby Henry.

As for the actual case, it was mismanaged by the social worker from the get-go. She messed this one up, plain and simple. There was no pressure from the court, or us, or Mom for Henry to be uprooted so immediately. Nothing had changed to disqualify Mom from all she had been working toward. She was still on plan and was close to finishing. She never hid bio Dad's identity and was upfront in the beginning about him. Even in a really good system, terrible things still happen. Cases are mismanaged, unfair rulings are made, and the children still sometimes lose. No system is perfect. And the people working within it are even less so. This caseworker, this time, was simply wrong.

There are so many amazing social workers out there. They do really hard work. They put in thankless, tireless hours. They are often put in lose-lose situations and have to make quick judgment calls. Henry's case is the only sour experience we have had within the foster care system so far. It was a tangled, knotty mess between birth mom, birth dad, and birth dad's extended family.

Regardless of our loss, there was no thought as to what was best for the child in this situation. He was ripped from his sister, from our family, and from his mom and grandma. Mom was within weeks of beginning to transition back to full custody. She was so close to reunifying, and instead, visitations slowed down and were made more complicated by the caseworker and birth dad. The caseworker pushed an agenda through based on the opportunity to unload a tricky case, which is in direct conflict with the positive, mandated changes made within the current foster system. The decisions made, and the treatment of our family, were the exact opposite of what DFS promotes. However, once the caseworker pushed the decision quietly through court, it was done, all in the name of keeping the peace with a loud, saber-rattling family. Foster moments like this are the moments that keep amazing families from opening their hearts and homes.

Walking Through Grief

On a personal level, losing baby Henry was the greatest loss I have ever known in my life. The sting of grief I felt from losing him was a thousand times more potent than any failed pregnancy or miscarriage. It stung more than all of those losses combined. In essence, a child had died, and there was no way for our family to tangibly reconcile the loss. There was no funeral. No memorial. No transition period. He was just gone! His high chair sat empty for weeks before I had the courage to put it away. I didn't go into his room for months. I just couldn't face the crib, the boxes of clothes that my friends lovingly packed away, and anything else that reminded me of him.

One of our favorite things to do together was to go to Danny's soccer practices. Henry loved to crawl after the balls and play on the ground. One particular day, while at the soccer field, Henry was eating animal crackers on my lap in the car. He wiped his cute, slobbery hands on my steering wheel, which left a little spot crusted over. I never washed it off. After Henry left, it stayed there for months and months. I just didn't have the heart to clean it. I felt as though washing it would wash him away with it. So I left it. Every time my thumb brushed over that part of the steering wheel, I cried.

My children who are pretty happy and easy-going most days were somber for several days. Each of them cried and grieved, even our oldest, Daniel. He was so attached to Henry. Everyone was. Henry was just that kind of baby. His spirit was so much bigger than his little body. Grace had a really hard time. The poor little thing already grieved for her mom every day. She was then separated from her brother, which made it worse. And I was emotionally lost, so comforting her was even more difficult. My sadness made her sad.

Losing Henry was the first time Adam had ever experienced real loss. He had lovingly walked by my side through all of our infertility challenges. He had been so patient, kind, loving, and supportive for many years. However, he played a supporting role in that story. Infertility was about me. He did not feel it or live it the same way I did. Because of this, when we lost Henry, I expected him to be the same steady stalwart that I had grown accustomed to. Boy, was I wrong.

I had never before in our marriage, and have never since, seen my husband in such sorrow and anguish. *He* cried every day. *He* felt emptiness deep down inside, the kind of ache that is squelched by nothing. I know that ache. Others who have lost significantly know it too. And for the first time, Adam understood the grief that I faced every time I had an ultrasound with no heartbeat. He finally knew what it felt like to carry that around. And all I wanted to do was take it away. Watching him grieve was so much worse than grieving myself because I knew exactly how he felt, and I knew that I couldn't make it better for him. Although I wanted to take his pain away, I was finally not alone. This bound us together in ways that I never knew were possible. It made our marriage stronger, our love deeper, and our devotion more fervent.

People have asked over the years how Adam dealt with our infertility. Many men suffer in silence as their partners garner most of the infertility attention based on simple biology. The same was true for us. The focus was always on me, especially in the beginning. Adam was really good at managing the problem and focusing on solutions. He was sad, of course, when we lost babies, especially the first year of miscarriages. But he was more upset that he couldn't fix this part of our marriage for me, that he couldn't give me what I so desperately wanted.

Adam said from the beginning, even before infertility, he didn't care how we had a family—bio, adopted, foster, whatever. It didn't matter to him; he just wanted me to be happy. Believing something before a trial is very different than believing that same thing during a trial. When infertility came our way, sure enough, he was true to his word. Losing a pregnancy did not devastate him. But losing Henry did. It shattered his heart into a thousand shards. I am pretty sure we bought out the Ben and Jerry's section of the grocery store that week, and the week after.

Grief turns to Healing

In time, as always, we emerged from the haze of grief over Henry with hearts full of gratitude. We put pictures of Henry up everywhere, including the kids' rooms. Some of the kids even put his picture in their binders so they could have him at school with them. Adam and I played videos for everyone so we could see him and remember the happy memories. We wrote in our journals, even the kids, so we would remember how this experience felt and how it was a blessing. Journaling helped us retain lessons learned and helped preserve our memories of Henry that would otherwise be forgotten. Somehow it didn't quite seem enough at the time, so we just kept putting one foot in front of the other holding tightly to each other as we slogged our way through the muck of grief.

Time heals most wounds. And as time went on for us, our overwhelming sorrow turned to warm memories and gratitude for the time we spent with Henry. It was tough walking through that loss with my kids. I was used to going through it on my own.

But this time, it wasn't just about me. I had to think about them too. Even though it was more complicated grieving with my family, it was also kind of nice to grieve with others for a change. Infertility loss is so isolating because your loved ones typically can't relate to how you are feeling. They feel bad, but don't actually feel the pain. The experience of losing Henry helped our entire family understand a little more about how difficult pregnancy loss was for me, and why having a baby was still a dream of mine. The children tangibly understood that having a baby wasn't about replacing them with DNA, but rather about the joy a baby could bring to our family and to our individual hearts.

LIFE LESSONS

Do Not Allow the What-Ifs to Stop You from Loving

It is always worth it! Although the experience of losing Henry was devastating, our entire family would do it over again. Any amount of grief and sorrow we felt in losing him was swallowed up in the privilege of knowing him! None of us would trade our memories of Henry for not having to experience the pain of letting go.

I cannot imagine those six months of my life, and every piece of joy we felt during that time, not existing. Loss is incredibly hard, but it allows us to know joy. Our family was not broken by the experience. We were made stronger, more complete. My children were given a deeper understanding of loss and grief and how they could use it to become stronger. This also brought us together as a family. We suffered together and we found gratitude together. It also prepared us for the next adventure of adding a bio baby to an adopted family. All of these blessings and many more not mentioned came to us because we took a risk. It did not end how we wanted it to, but it was certainly worth it.

Do not let the fear of losing a foster child or adoption placement stop you from gaining a Henry in your life. Knowing him was worth losing him. If fostering or adopting has been sitting in your heart for a while, or maybe even as you read this book, I can make only one promise. It is worth the price you pay to open your home and your heart. You have nothing to lose, and absolutely everything to gain. It is hard, really hard. It is messy and complicated and sometimes devastating, but the child's happiness is way more important than our temporary discomfort. Don't let fear stop you from loving in whatever form that takes for your family!

Chapter Six

In-vitro Makes an Entrance

June 21, 2012

So I was standing at the kitchen counter last night staring, staring, staring. Yes, staring at the packet of birth control pills wondering what the heck I was supposed to do with it. Seriously! Luckily, I have a sister or two very familiar with birth control. Being the Fertile Myrtles that they are, they helped me match up the sticker strip to the pill package. And voila, I am a birth control virgin no longer. That's kind of weird. Okay, a lot weird. But weirder still is that I found myself in a random blood lab in a random city doing a time-sensitive blood draw so Dr. Fisch can create my IVF protocol. It was déjà vu because I have been in multiple states in multiple blood labs doing multiple blood draws over the years, but always because of miscarriage. Adam and I always seemed to be traveling when I would miscarry. So it was kind of ironic that I was now getting my blood drawn to try to get pregnant. We haven't been pregnant since 2010 that I know of, and we stopped pursuing fertility options when we started adopting in 2007, so I feel like a fish out of water. But if we don't do it now . . .

Being thirty-six, I qualify for the "under thirty-eight" plan. Isn't that great? Ha! That means a gracious $3,000 is knocked off the top. But we all know how expensive IVF can be. We won't know our true cost until we find out what drug protocol I'll be on. Are we hopeful? A little. Do we feel like we'll get a baby? Not really. Do we want to KNOW so we can move on? Yes! And when my sweet Annie crawls in bed with me after losing our foster baby, Henry, and says, "Mommy, I want another baby, but one that doesn't go away," we feel like we have to try. It's now or never!

After losing Henry, I felt compelled pretty immediately to begin IVF treatments. Adam was concerned that the idea was a very expensive rebound that would yield nothing but more heartache, but I knew it wasn't just a rebound decision. The experience with Henry only strengthened the baby feeling that had slowly crept back into my heart as we parented Henry and Grace. My biological clock wasn't just ticking, it was pounding, and I had the sense that it was literally now or never. IVF was a pretty expensive and invasive favor to ask of Adam, but he chose to act in faith this time (it was usually me doing the faith thing) and got on board. For him, the decision was purely driven by his desire to make me happy. He had no real need to attach DNA to his name. I L-O-V-E that about him.

The decision for me was much more complicated. Although I was firm in my resolve to try, pursuing IVF left me feeling immense amounts of guilt over the cost of treatment and guilt over leaving parentless children without a home. I felt as if I was somehow sacrificing them to pursue a selfish desire. After all the time that had passed, with all the children who needed homes, why was I going back to square one? Why would I spend money on a procedure that I consciously shunned six years prior; a procedure that only has a 40% success rate?

After much meditation and prayer, the answer became clear and simple: a baby! It no longer had anything to do with DNA or wanting the pregnancy experience or even thinking it would fill some hole that was missing? Two or three years previously that would have definitely been the case. It was simply and beautifully about bringing a baby into our home for our whole family to enjoy.

With seven children living in the home, adopting a healthy newborn through a private adoption was all but out of reach. Yes, we could have taken multiple placements from foster care and eventually adopted an infant, but how many years and how many Henries would I have to say goodbye to in the process? We were not opposed to continuing down the foster care path. In fact, we saw ourselves continuing to foster, perhaps adopting at least once more regardless of our fertility outcome. However, all of our children were still reeling from losing their foster brother and sister. They *really* wanted me to have a baby. And I simply felt like it was the right time.

We were quickly led to the right doctor this time around, which confirmed my female intuition. Dr. Jeffrey Fisch (Green Valley Fertility Partners) in Las Vegas, Nevada, is who we decided to see. He was a cool, refreshing breeze blowing through the parched desert of Vegas fertility doctors, the antithesis of everything we had previously experienced with fertility clinics in our city. He was kind, thoughtful, open, and reasonable. Dr. Fisch was able to be direct without being hurtful. We never felt like a number. And even though he was super confident in his abilities, with a track record to prove it, he was not arrogant.

He gave me his mobile number, which he trusted I would only use in a true emergency.

In addition to liking Dr. Fisch, we also liked his staff. His nurses did an amazing job assuaging fears without giving false hope. Imagine the many frantic phone calls they regularly field, phone calls from hormonally unhinged, hopeful mommies who are freaking out about not taking a pill on time, missing a shot, etc. The staff at GVFP was exceptional. I knew I was in the right place.

IVF Inner Workings

August 7, 2012

Just under three weeks until we transfer a hoped for little McCracken.

Step 1. birth control, check

Step 2. six days of Lupron injections and start a daily dose of dexamethasone, check

Step 3. 13 days of Ganirelix injections, starting tomorrow

Other awesome pokes and pills to look forward to: Follistim injections, hCG injection, folic acid pill, And of course the regular ultrasounds... beginning on 8/13

Probable Egg Retrieval–8/24... yes, back to school night. Really?

Probable Embryo Transfer–8/27... yes, first day of school. Yep. That's my life.

AWESOME!!!

We will know on Labor Day if we're pregnant.

From beginning consultation to embryo transfer it can take up to three months for a full round of in-vitro. It involves chart tracking, drug protocols, tiny shots in the tummy, and very large shots in the butt. The week leading up to egg retrieval and embryo transfer requires stimulation medication, which is pretty brutal on the body, physically. It is definitely the most difficult portion of the process.

Egg retrieval week is filled with intense bloating and cramping as the ovaries and hormones necessary to grow one's eggs work overtime to mature as many eggs as possible, all at once. The pain of this process gets progressively worse as the ovaries are pumped full of estrogen and the follicles grow in size. To put it in perspective for the female reader, imagine your very worst period, the worst bloating, the worst cramping, the worst sore achiness that you have experienced. It's like that, but worse.

By the seventh day of our last week, I could barely stand upright; the pain in my right ovary, which was where the majority of my growing eggs were located, was greater than any pain of any impending miscarriage. After all these years, my palms still sweat and I get a little dizzy when I think about that week. I kept reminding myself during that painful week that it was not another miscarriage happening, but rather a really good thing that could help yield a baby. I don't think I ever quite convinced myself.

Two nights before my retrieval procedure, Adam and I went on a double date with our friends, Rob and Jaime. They wanted to take my mind off of things and we all *love* chocolate so naturally we decided to hit the chocolate bar at Caesar's Palace to end our date night. I do not remember much about that night except the very long walk through the casino and down the promenade. I was certain a sharp, hot knife was slicing through my ovaries with every step.

What was I thinking? My first mistake was that I wore jeans. Dumb. Who wears tight jeans when they are having the most intense, prolonged period of their life? My second mistake was that I wore heels, which made the pain much worse. There was no give in my step and my body ached with every forward-moving inch. I am pretty sure my friends walked several paces ahead because my hobbled steps and loud groans were ridiculously embarrassing. I would have walked ahead of me too if I could! By the time we arrived at dessert, I could not stand up straight having to be steadied by Adam. I was sure both of my ovaries would burst open at any moment right there in the restaurant. Needless to say, I really needed my own delicious plate of all things chocolate that night. I did not share!

Egg Retrieval

Egg retrieval requires general anesthesia, as the procedure is quite painful. Strapped to a bed with my legs secured high in the air, I felt as if I was attached to some medieval torture chamber. The table I was on was similar to one used for pelvic exams, except that the stirrups were larger and for my legs, not for my feet. Black leather straps were tied around each of my legs as well as the stirrups to keep my legs in place. Thankfully, before I knew it, the anesthesiologist had given me the good stuff and I was off dreaming of carpools and soccer practice and all things back-to-school related.

During the procedure, the doctors guide a tube with a tiny needle up through the vaginal canal and past the uterus landing it right next to the ovary. The needle then makes a tiny hole in the ovary and sucks the eggs out. Amazing, right?

I woke up a little while later, Adam safely back at my side in the recovery bay. He was not with me during the procedure as he had his own contribution to give to this baby-making process.

My procedure was scheduled for 9:30, and we were home by 1:00. I was prepared by a few friends to expect pain and to take it easy. Some women are ready to go back to work after 24 hours. I find that unbelievable. Dr. Fisch clarified this discrepancy by indicating that the more eggs retrieved, the longer the recovery time can be. Some women's recovery can take up to three or four days depending on the intensity of the procedure. I had low to moderate pain (about a three on the pain scale) when I woke up from surgery. I was at a five or six by the time I was home and settled. Not too bad considering the amount of eggs that were retrieved.

The Outcome

I had many mature follicles with 23 eggs ready to burst out of me by the time retrieval day came. Some women only have one or two follicles and only one or two or three eggs retrieved. I was supposed to retrieve on Friday or Saturday, but because I had so many eggs, most of them were not stimulated quite enough so the doctor had to keep "cooking" me a bit. Translation—more stimulation meds, more trips to the pharmacy, more money, and more pokes in my belly. Hence, the weekend date night scene from hell at Caesar's Palace.

Logic would suggest that the more eggs one produces, the more viable embryos. This is not typically the case, however. Most women who produce a lot of eggs suffer from diminished egg quality, which was what happened with me. Even when a lot of eggs are retrieved, very few embryos usually survive the incubation and fertilization process. This can be frustrating and heart-breaking for IVF patients as they watch their number of eggs and embryos dwindle throughout fertilization week.

Of the 23 eggs they retrieved from me on a Sunday, 17 had fertilized by Monday morning. By that

Wednesday, we had only 10 left. And by the end of the week, there was a small handful of precious "good embryos," six to be exact. As my sweet doctor would always say, however, it only takes one good egg to make a baby. And we had six. I had absolutely nothing to complain about.

Embryos Away

On 31August 2011, two little embryos were implanted in my uterus. Unlike egg retrieval, this procedure was relatively short and painless. Well, I did have an ice cold speculum (yes, they ice it first) inserted so that a catheter could reach all the way to my uterus. Dr. Fisch then used the catheter to guide the embryos into their proper place.

There is no sedation for a transfer, although I was given a Valium about 30 minutes before the procedure took place. I did not feel any relaxing or numbing effects from the medicine, but then again, maybe it would have been more painful if I hadn't had anything at all. I don't care to find out.

Adam was able to be in the room for this procedure and we were able to view the whole thing on the screen of the ultrasound machine. I was so grateful to have his hand. After going through the egg retrieval, I was scared this would be just as bad. I am pretty sure Adam has a few tiny scars from my fingernail marks left on his forearm that day.

After I was prepped for transfer, Dr. Fisch opened the door to the embryology lab and the embryologist brought the tube forward that had our potential babies inside. Yeah, that was a little weird. And cool. He verified that I was who I said I was and that my name was on the tube as to avoid a monumental mix-up.

After loading the embryos into the catheter tube, Dr. Fisch guided each embryo up the tiny catheter line with great skill and finesse. My second embryo got stuck in the tube, which is common. The embryologist took the tube back in the lab to verify and reload the second little embryo. Dr. Fisch said it was a "sticky one," which could be good. I held onto that as I continued to crush my husband's arm beside me. The second attempt was successful and both embryos were buried inside my uterine lining.

The whole procedure took about 20 minutes, quick and easy. The best part of the whole thing was when Dr. Fisch drew a little heart around the embryos on the ultrasound. He was amazing through the whole process. He didn't just leave the room as soon as the transfer was complete. Instead, he walked over to my side, grabbed my hands, and then rubbed my belly with one hand while clinging to his little Kokopelli (fertility deity) charm that he wears around his neck with his other hand, rubbing it for good luck. He then reminded us, and himself, that he had done his best and the rest was in God's hands. Lastly, he hugged us. Amazing! He didn't need to do that, but it made all the difference for someone who had just put all her money, hopes, and body parts literally in his hands.

I could not have asked for better care on all accounts. No matter the outcome, we knew we were in the right place at the right time with the right people caring for us. No regrets!

More Loss

I remember when our first transfer yielded a pregnancy. How could I forget?

November 8, 2012

We did get pregnant. The transfer worked. We saw a heartbeat at seven weeks. We saw another heartbeat, and growing baby, at eight and a half weeks. We went in at ten weeks for a final ultrasound before we were to be sent off to the regular OB. No heartbeat! The baby had died a few days before. D&C performed the next day. That was three weeks ago.

We started with two sacs. One stopped progressing and was passed around eight weeks. It did not harm the other baby, so we are still stumped as to the cause of this miscarriage. Everything looked great. We were measuring on target. Strong heartbeat. Religious about my meds and hormones. In fact, the doctor's face dropped at the ultrasound, completely perplexed. He had brought us into the big room with the nice monitor so he could play around a bit and enjoy our last visit. Needless to say, he was just as shocked as we were. Dr. Fisch suggested a D&C so we could test the fetus for abnormalities. I went with his recommendation, and am glad I did. I have always passed pregnancies naturally, but this time was different, and I have no regrets about taking care of it immediately.

We will get the results of the fetal testing at our consult next week. We'll see where we go from here. If the tests come back normal, we're not sure what changes will be made, but we'll at least know if that was the cause. For now, I take great comfort in knowing we actually had a growing baby in a sac in the right spot with all its parts. That is something that we haven't had before. The loss stings more because of this, for sure. But we are hopeful that we are one step closer to having a baby.

Our prayer now is that our frozen embryos are chromosomally normal and viable. That at least one of the four of them survives the thaw and makes it to term. We'll probably cycle in December or January. I'm not sure how many more losses I can take this year. It's a GOOD thing 2012 is drawing to a close! :)

Losing a baby that was implanted in the correct place and healthily growing on schedule was new and different for me. It wasn't just an idea of a baby that I lost this time, but an expectation that this was the one. For the first time in a decade of trying, things seemed to be swinging our way. There was no physical warning with this loss. The growing baby was simply dead. The emotional effects of the fertility drugs and the exorbitant cost of treatments added to my devastation. Compared to others' pregnancy losses, this was *only* a ten-week loss, but if I have learned anything throughout the years, it is that loss is loss. Period! No one should apologize for feeling it. And no one should feel pressured to "get over it" in any certain time frame. Instead, we should rally around those who have lost. And if it takes a little longer for some than for others, the rallying should continue. Grief has no time limit, no set re-entry to normalcy. Grief changes our spirits, thereby changing the relationships around us. For me, losing babies grew my understanding for those who have experienced any kind of loss. It grew my compassion and my ability to help others grieve.

In classy Dr. Fisch style, he did not cart us off to a hospital. The clinic performed the D&C at their office, which was a thousand times better. No going to the pregnancy floor at the hospital. No putting my body in someone else's hands that had no idea what we had just gone through. Dr. Fisch performed the procedure himself. And the same staff that helped us become pregnant mourned our loss with us. These are moments that are never forgotten. Losing a baby in this way gave us the courage to try again.

We knew we were not alone and that we were in the best possible hands.

By February 2013, Adam and I had gained enough courage to transfer again. I just wanted to get the trying over with because I knew we were done with paying to harvest more eggs. Shockingly, both embryos made the thaw and implanted beautifully. Again! This time our hCG numbers increased much more rapidly than with the first transfer. Because of this, Dr. Fisch felt like it was the one. I, on the other hand, prepared my heart for another baby loss.

Sweet Angel Baby
and Other Angels

As excited as we were for this pregnancy, we also made the crazy decision to take a foster placement of three little girls three and under. They were legally free for adoption and the placement kind of just fell into our laps. I was pretty afraid of losing our pregnancy and figured maybe this was God hedging our bets for us. So we met them and decided to say yes. Plus, we had always felt like there was one more adoption out there for our family, but we had no idea when or how it would present itself. Maybe this was it.

Foster parenting is full of surprises at every twist and turn. The day before we were set to pick the girls up permanently, our caseworker called with news that the girls had a two-month-old baby brother. Were we willing to take him too? Um, yes!

So we picked the four of them up and I fell instantly in love with Baby K. The girls were beautiful and super sweet, and I knew I would grow to love them, but this angel baby was simply a dream straight out of heaven. His temperament was the kind every parent hopes for. Baby K had deliciously rich skin, chocolaty perfect in every way. He had dark, beautiful ringlets throughout his hair that I would sit and twirl for hours while cooing him to sleep. Snuggling him was the sweet healing recipe my soul needed to soothe the miscarriage fears swirling all around me. Conditioned to expect loss, I was simultaneously hopeful and discouraged.

Ironically, the night we brought the children home, I had a terrible bleeding episode accompanied by horrific cramping. Adam and I sat on the bathroom floor huddled together crying, sure that we were miscarrying. Again! We went in the next day for an almost seven-week ultrasound, fully expecting bad news. Dr. Fisch was prepared to confirm the news as he began the scan. I lay on the table softly sobbing as I tightly squeezed Adam's hand, not daring to open my eyes or even breathe.

Dr. Fisch did not say anything for what seemed like an eternity. Instead, he continued to probe and scan in bleak silence. Finally, he directed us to the monitor, turning on the sound so we could hear the heart that still faintly beat inside of me. Miracles happen. Instead of an empty sac, we discovered a tiny little fetus with a tiny but healthy heartbeat.

There was no known reason for the threatened miscarriage except the stress I had been under with getting ready for our new arrivals and getting our large family ready to move several states away. Terrible nausea and sickness progressed rapidly with this early pregnancy. I was ordered to stay down as much as possible, which was simply not going to happen with so many little ones who needed my care.

As we left the doctor's office in total shock, I feared I would need to say goodbye to our new foster babies. The problem was that I did not want to. Who lets go of a legally-free sibling group of such sweet little ones? It is not in my nature to give up, or in Adam's. After several days of pondering, prayer, and meditation, though, I knew I needed to let go, and I knew that Adam would not do it. He had been conditioned to think we would eventually lose the pregnancy, and he did not want to risk losing the adoption too. Who could blame him? I certainly couldn't. And I could not ask him to make the phone call, but I knew it needed to be done.

Even if this pregnancy failed, we had another shot with two more embryos waiting in deep freezer and I was clearly over my limit on what I could give during this time, which had never happened before. Against Adam's vote and against my desire to keep our sweet angel babies, I nervously called the social worker to give our notice. The instant I hung up the phone, I felt an enormous amount of relief and peace wash over me. It was the right and best thing for everyone, especially for the little ones, who deserved the full attention of a mother and father.

Adam was devastated, and we were at a true impasse. There was a wide crevasse of hostility wedged in between us, and we were having a difficult time reaching each other. For a few days, I actually wondered if this would break our steel-plated marriage. We were together, but not really. It was a new feeling for me. With all other family-related decisions, we had moved forward as a united front. We were not always on the same page, but we were at least in the same chapter or book. This time was distinctly different. Adam was paralyzed by the decision because he had made a commitment to these sweet little ones. In all of his infinite optimism, he felt like we could do it, that it would be super hard, but that we could get through. He would not allow himself to consider that we might have to make a choice. His self-admitted myopic view closed him off to seeing my needs and the needs of the fragile pregnancy. For the first and only time in our marriage, I pulled the woman card and chose the pregnancy.

I chose the pregnancy! I knew it would certainly fail if I kept the sibling group, but I had a shot if I didn't. How does one make that decision? How does someone who has devoted her life to adoption and sibling groups send a placement back in hopes of having a baby? Selfishness and shame began to creep into my heart. I placed ALL of my faith into a very tiny offering basket and threw it toward Heaven. It was a Hail Mary at best. What if the pregnancy failed anyway? Would I be able to live with the guilt? What about Adam? Would he resent me forever for losing the placement with nothing to show for it? The last thing I needed was to be stuck in a deep marriage valley.

After I chucked that basket of faith as high as it could go, tender knowledge from above was granted to me. I knew it would work out, that my husband would come around, and that things would be better for everyone than I could yet imagine.

We thought for sure the kids would be placed into foster care while an adoptive resource was found, which continued breaking my heart. But within three days of giving our notice, a family's profile popped up with open beds. *Three Days*. This family had been waiting for an adoptive placement for two years. They were also the same religion as us, which meant a lot considering we thought of the kids as ours. The children's forever mom and I were able to transfer from my house to hers easily and with a smooth transition for the children. She took the three older girls for a week and asked if I would keep the baby while she prepared everything. I will forever treasure that gifted week with Baby K. He brought light to my life and joy to the children.

Our time with Baby K reminded us all why we were trying to have a baby. It was painful to give him to another family, but not as difficult as when we lost Henry. We had time to say goodbye properly and let go in a sweet way. It was everything that our transfer with Henry was not. Baby K received the opportunity to be raised with his sisters in an excellent home, out of the system. My heart wishes that for every child, biological or adopted!

Our caseworker was understandably disappointed at first, but as things played out she was grateful we initially took the kids, regardless. The children were able to be reunited in our home. Actually, it was the first time the girls even knew about their baby brother. All four were transferred from suboptimal placements to us, together. We were honored to help while their new forever home was being prepared.

Through all of our crazy family-building adventures, our circle of influence has been unparalleled. In this case, it was my dad who deserved the superhero cape. He flew down for the week in my mom's place, as I was on strict bed rest and could not meet the new children's physical needs as there were four under four, three of which slept in cribs. He helped take care of the little girls so Adam could go to work. He cooked, cleaned, changed diapers, played, rocked, etc. He was the foster babies' dad and mom the week before the transition. It was difficult for him to let them go, even though he knew it was right. I know exactly how he felt when he helped put them in the car to wave goodbye for the very last time.

I am extra grateful for his sacrifice of love and service on our behalf. My dad quite literally saved my pregnancy through his service that week. I *know* he did. Through my dad, and others, God's hand was once again in our home, tangibly moving and healing us through a most difficult moment. In the end, and with a few weeks of healing behind us, Adam recognized the wisdom in letting the babies go, and I released the guilt I had over my flourishing pregnancy. We felt honored to be small instruments in helping little ones who could not help themselves. Once again, it was worth it! For us, it was time to take a break from foster care and focus on nurturing the thriving pregnancy we had waited so long to experience.

Hannah

Our eighth little miracle arrived via emergency C-section at thirty weeks and three days. Not exactly the joyful birth we had envisioned, but that was par for the course in our family-growing experience. We were not surprised. After spending my first trimester on bed rest and my second trimester helping my children adjust to our new home and life in Washington State, I developed pre-eclampsia at twenty-eight weeks. At twenty-nine weeks I was admitted to the hospital for the rest of my pregnancy. One week later, my blood pressure could no longer be controlled with medication. In a rush to save me and the baby, my doctor and her team frantically prepared to operate. Drugged and confused, they wheeled me to surgery, and before I knew what was really happening, my mind went dark.

When I awoke, Adam was able to deliver the sweet news that our baby had survived. She was nameless, but alive. She weighed two pounds eight ounces and was perfect in every way. When she was born, she was so small that her daddy's wedding ring fit all the way up her tiny stick of an arm. I did not get to see her for a few days, as I was still on the mag drag (magnesium), as the nurses called it, to keep my blood pressure stable.

My miracle-working OB reported to Adam that on a scale of one to ten, my pre-eclampsia was an eleven, and it was going to take at least a week before they would consider releasing me from the hospital. In the meantime, magnesium was my friend. It is very effective at controlling blood pressure, but with that, all other metabolic functions are slowed as well. Standing up and even opening my eyes was nearly impossible. Let's just say I was seeing purple unicorns float across the room in slow motion for a couple of days.

I was not allowed to see our baby during this time, as I could not even sit in a wheelchair to be taken down to the NICU. Gratefully, I was so out of it that I barely remembered having a baby. Adam was a total rock star, managing mother and child, both of whom were fighting to recover.

During my convalescence, I was instructed by the lactation specialists to pump colostrum. Really?!? I could barely remember the specialist coming into the room, let alone teaching me how to use the hospital pump. Not to mention that I was still supposed to be pregnant. Breastfeeding had not made my to-do list yet, so it caught me completely off guard. I am certain that watching me fiddle and fumble with that foreign contraption was just as comical to the specialists as the purple unicorns had become to me. Somehow, with the help of my mom and husband, we made things work, and the baby got what she needed.

After a couple of days, I told Adam to choose one of the baby names off our list. I needed her to have a name, as I was still unable to meet her. The next time he went down to deliver her milk, Adam settled on the name Hannah, which was the perfect name for a baby who had been purposefully prayed for by so many. It also happened to be my favorite name on the list.

When I was finally allowed to see Hannah for the first time, it was like coming home. There is no other way to describe it. As Adam wheeled me to her Isolette (incubator), I felt a rushing tidal wave of love wash over me. I had only experienced that rush one other time—when I held our foster son Henry for the first time. This was that same exact feeling, only better, because I knew with certainty we were able to keep her. She was a part of our family, forever! Hannah's fingers, toes, nose, lips, everything about her was perfection. Never mind the tubes and wires and the little mask that covered her eyes, she was beautiful. Her little body was so fragile, so tiny, and so helpless. Skin-to-skin contact with our pop-can-sized miracle as she lay nestled on my chest validated every decision and sacrifice we made to get her here.

Going home from the hospital without Hannah was not what I envisioned in my mommy dreams. My hormones were all messed up and my faculties had not completely returned, but I knew as sure as the sun rises that Hannah was yet another miracle sent to our family, a pure gift from above. This truth was verified over and over as the children were able to see her from the hospital window week after week. Their little heads would bob up and down, stealing glances—sweet, futile attempts to try to get the two pounder's attention. They couldn't believe she was real, and all they wanted to do was hold her. They believed she was their miracle. I believed it too!

We spent eight weeks and countless hours watching our sweet miracle grow in the special area of the hospital, the NICU. She would not have lived without the care given from our now favorite NICU nurses. Their attention, kindness, and competence were unparalleled. In the little spare time they had, I received notes "written" from Hannah to me, I received pictures of Hannah when they would dress her in the cute outfits I would leave, and I was given a special little nook by the window once Hannah was out of her Isolette so when the kids would come to visit they had the best possible view. What started out as a traumatic experience ended up being one of my favorite memories. Hannah's NICU stay was definitely difficult as I tried to manage my other children and our new life in Washington, but my whole family rallied to help, allowing me to spend most of the days and evenings with our sweet, new blessing.

Once Hannah was released, the children were finally able to hold her for the very first time. She was still so tiny, just under five pounds, and they were so caring and gentle with her. No jealousy, no sadness, just joy and gratitude that she was finally home.

After losing Henry, our family realized that it didn't matter where the baby came from. They could love a bio baby the same as a foster baby or an adopted baby or a cousin or whatever. Love is love. And my adopted children loved Hannah. They still love her. Actually, they dote on her in the most annoying ways. We have the most well adjusted, blended family in that way. It is possible! Hannah obviously sees no difference. Her brown-skinned siblings are all she knows.

The experiences our children have had helping to raise Hannah coupled with their knowledge of our unconditional love for each of them keeps all of us rooted and blossoming in our love-grown family. If it wasn't for our adopted children, we would probably never know our biological daughter. They pushed her here. They prayed for her. They encouraged me. They supported my decision to try to save the baby, sacrificing their new little foster sisters. Their faith was stronger than mine, at every turn. I hope they continue to realize that they are *all* miracles to me!

To Try or not to Try

When Hannah was one, and despite severe discouragement from three specialists, we tried one last embryo transfer. Looking back, it was really selfish of me to try knowing that I was at increased risk for complications and/or death. My body was approaching forty though and there were two little embryos sitting in a deep freezer somewhere. All I could envision was Hannah's sweet face. What if we had left *her* in the freezer?

Adam still has PTSD when we discuss my hospital stay and delivery, with every reason to be freaked out. He witnessed all the scary. Adam listened to my monitors continually going off in the last few hours before delivery because they couldn't control my blood pressure, even with the magnesium. He watched me pass out on the table after they messed up the epidural TWICE (thank goodness they finally just put me to sleep). He observed the doctors frantically tear into me to get the baby out, unsure that I could handle the anesthesia. He held his own breath when Hannah came out not breathing and the NICU team rushed to aid her. His view pretty much sucked. All I remembered were the dancing unicorns. Needless to say, we were both relieved that our last IVF attempt failed. We could finally put fertility treatments completely behind us.

LIFE LESSONS

Cast a Wide Net

Casting a wide net is paramount to living a life full of faith, joy, and purpose. If we had not said yes to the foster/adoption placement of the four sweet angel babies, even when the logical thing to do was to say no, that darling little sibling group would have stayed separated from each other for a very long time and might not have received an adoptive home together.

This illustration does not mean we should say yes to every opportunity. We personally have said no many times. However, we keep ourselves open and ready in case an opportunity presents itself. Time after time we have seen others blessed and moved into positive positions because we were simply ready. Ready to help. Ready to act. Ready to do. For Adam and me, that has meant moving forward with adoptions we were not quite sure about, getting our foster license even though we were not exactly sure we would ever take a placement, and also taking placements when we were not sure why we were doing it. It looks different for everyone. The point is to live our lives wide open, preparing our hearts to be ready, and then acting when it feels right. God, or the universe, or the ethos, whatever spiritual theory you subscribe to, cannot use us if we do not want to be used.

Casting wide in all aspects of our lives is what gives us access to the boundless opportunities and endless rewards that circle all around us, but we have to cast the net. We must cast! We cannot just stand on the shore thinking about it. Fear keeps us stationary. If we do not move forward, then we do not progress. Period. We cannot effect change. We cannot seize significant moments for ourselves and others. Purpose-driven opportunities are not gained by standing around on the shoreline hoping they magically crawl into our nets.

The most spectacular times of growth, movement, and joy for our family have come only after making the decision to cast into the deepest of waters, sometimes casting ourselves straight into the darkness of a raging sea. Releasing ourselves from the shore along with our nets has yielded bounty every single time. The good bounty of softened minds, healed hearts, and changed lives. And that, my friends, is a net worth casting!

Just Go for It

Life is too short. We will almost never regret doing something and failing, but we will often regret never trying. Hannah has Adam wrapped so tightly around every single one of his fingers that it is kind of ridiculous. Needless to say, he is pretty happy that we went for fertility treatments. He did it for me, but he would do it again now that he has experienced having a baby. We would not know that if we had not tried. It was expensive, really expensive, like $30,000 expensive. There were no guarantees, none. In fact, the odds were really low that our procedure would yield a baby. Regardless, we went for it.

If we had failed in our IVF attempts, there would still be no regrets. My questions and hopes would have been answered either way. I know that is true because we went for it again, shelling out another $7,000 to try with the last of our frozen embryos. Although we were beyond sad that neither of the embryos made it past implantation, we could see the tender mercy in not having to face another high-risk pregnancy or another NICU stay. The point is that we went for it. Just like we went for both of our adoptions, uncertain of the outcome, or like we went for other placements and adoption options that didn't pan out. It is the life in our years that matters. If we had continued to just think about adopting, we would still be childless. Whatever it is that you want to do, stop fence-sitting and just go for it!

CHAPTER SEVEN

Adoption Is Not the Same

Adoption is not the same as creating life. It just isn't. I know there are many people who disagree, but just because we want it to be the same does not make it true. Adoption is amazing. It has certainly fulfilled me and added significant joy to my life, but I never thought adoption by itself would fill the hole inside me that longed to grow life. Even though adoption is a second option for some, it is certainly not second best. It is just different. There is no reason to apologize or make excuses for that fact. Things don't have to be the same to be equally joyful.

I knew that when we finally brought our kids home, my fertility woes would not disappear, that the previous four and a half years of disappointment and loss would not miraculously be erased. I always assumed there would be an emptiness of sorts that remained, regardless of our full arms and happy family life.

Even still, I hoped. I hoped that our four children, and then seven, would not just fill my empty arms completely, but fill the desire inside my heart to have a baby. I hoped I would no longer be jealous of my friends' ultrasound pictures. I hoped that my offerings of grace and goodness would overshadow the loneliness and isolation infertility brings.

To be painfully honest, that did not happen. In fact, just the opposite occurred. Others might think I do not love my adopted children enough or that adoption might be wrong for them based on my experience. I hope the love I have for my children proves that is not true. My children are my heart. They are everything to me. I find copious amounts of joy in raising them and loving them. I believe they find the same joy and love in me.

A private chamber of my heart that was all my own though, a tiny part that I shared with no one else, still longed to have a baby. It was fine. It didn't paralyze me and didn't steal joy from the family I had. But it was there, ever so softly beating deep inside.

After the adoptions, when friends would talk about their pregnancy plans it would still sting just as much as before. Because you see, they could do that. They could decide if and when and how they would have a baby. They could decide when to "start trying" so that it fit perfectly with their summer vacation or their debt payment plan or their educational goals. And sure, there is risk involved with every pregnancy. Miscarriage happens a lot. It is risky business for sure, but the risk seemed much less for my fertile friends. An adoptive mother wrote a beautiful letter to me outlining her experiences with pregnancy and adoption just before we left for Bogotá. I thank her for sharing so openly.

> **"The thing that [name removed] really taught me is that pregnancy is not that big of a deal. That you love your bio kids the same as you love your adopted kids. That color or blood ties really do not matter. Pregnancy, nursing, babies are so temporary, they are gone in a blink, but motherhood is eternal. Being a mother is what matters... The hope that once your children are home and settled and healed, you will love them so much that you would not want to be a mother any other way. You will actually be glad that you had infertility because it gave you your children. You will be glad that it cost so much and took so long because it helped you appreciate them all the more."**

I, unfortunately, did not feel the same. Yes, I was grateful that infertility led me down the path of adoption. I appreciate the opportunity to be a parent more than anything in the whole world. And yes, I do believe that being a mother is what matters most. However, if this world ran as it should, there would be no orphans. There would be no need for adoption. Children wouldn't suffer. Biological families would be together, forever. I will never be grateful for the "opportunity" to pay $40,000 to adopt. It's an insane amount of money that I would pay all over again, but I am not grateful that we spent it. Nor do I think my children should ever be grateful that their first families fell apart. The agony of childless arms was enough for me to appreciate my kids. Adoption is a beautiful answer, but no one should wish it existed.

After many years of adoption and miscarriages and a semi-successful pregnancy, I still believe that for those who desire it, having a baby is a very big deal. My personal struggle to find grace and to be gracious in the midst of adversity is a true hallmark of my journey to and through motherhood. I am not perfect, but I sure try to be my best. I wish desperately that I had given birth to my seven adopted angels that bless our home. I wish that I had been with them since conception. I wish that they did not endure the things they did while waiting for someone new to love them. I will always wish that they had come to me another way, that I had been the one to hold them and rock them and watch them take their first steps. And I find no shame in admitting that.

For me, pregnancy was never about DNA; it was always about the biological experience. And no one should feel guilty for wanting to experience it, even those of us who have adopted. Would we wish for our adopted children to be infertile? No! I will always wish for the experience of bringing more life into this world. And that is totally okay!

Bonding in Progress

What if you don't love them? What if you don't like them? How do you love someone you don't know? How can you bring a stranger into your home and actually enjoy it? I have been asked these questions and others so many times over the years. Usually, they are well-meaning and come from a place of love, even if poorly delivered. Most people have legitimate questions. Heck, I wonder all kinds of things when I see a "different" family walking down the street, and I am one! Curiosity is a primal part of human nature and should not be approached as hostile unless it is clear that motives are malicious. Curious questions provide a wonderful opportunity to advocate for children, to share stories, and to promote understanding.

The answer to most bonding questions is so simple, really. All relationships are grown. Every relationship is unique. DNA based or not, unconditional love develops over time and through experience. We have different relationships with each of our children, our parents, our brothers and sisters, our friends. Fostering and adopting are no different. Some people we will naturally bond with, and others we won't. That is a part of real life and real family.

Many parents have highly dysfunctional relationships with perfectly normal, biological children. Most kids within family units are bio kids, which means that most messed-up adults grew up in biological families. We nurture each other's nature, but our natural tendencies and personalities are ours, no matter who birthed us.

I am wholly and completely bonded to several of my adopted kids just as I am to Hannah, with no difference in the depth of my bond. I do love my adopted kids differently than Hannah, however. Our relationships were grown in different ways. To profess there is no difference is to peddle a lie wrapped up in a warm, fuzzy unicorn blanket. Just because the relationships are different does not make our love or bond any less real or beautiful or fulfilling. I wouldn't trade my adopted kids and our special mother-child relationships for a million Hannahs. I certainly wish I had birthed each of them, but only so I would have more time with them, so their tender, early lives would not have been so terrible.

Sometimes bonding with a child is as natural as breathing, like our family's attachment to baby Henry. Other times, it takes years to feel completely bonded, or even partially so. One of my children has spent our whole relationship on my "I need to work harder on bonding with this child" list. It isn't what I imagined it would be in the beginning. Some relationships just take much longer to cultivate.

One thing I know for certain though is that I am not a failure because we are still working on bonding and attachment all these years later. I take care of this child's needs, give opportunities, and provide protection. I would lay down my life for this child as I would for any of our children. This particular relationship is *Work* with a big, fat capital W. I imagine it will continue to be that way into adulthood. This child has made insane amounts of progress over the past two years providing us much hope for a very warm and bright future.

I work really hard at growing my own ability to love and have compassion. My children have helped me become more this way over time, but it has been a constant work in progress for me. Not all of my love-grown relationships have been like the one with Henry. Sometimes bonding, depending on the child I am working with, takes dedicated focus just as with the child above.

Instant bonding is much easier for Adam than for me. He can just look at a picture and be attached. When I looked at that very first picture of our Colombians, knowing they were mine, knowing it was right, feeling like I would do anything to protect and defend the children in that picture, all came from a place of commitment and duty and hope for the future. I took a chance. And I have no regrets. But there were certainly no guarantees either. You get what you get. As with deciding to have a baby, you just have to be all in and love whatever is on the other side like crazy even when you don't feel like it and especially when you receive no reciprocation from the child.

My kiddos came from some scary backgrounds, and they are so awesome. They just are. They are happy, grateful, beautiful kids. I dedicated myself to training them, but all I really did was give them opportunities for their natures to shine through. I loved them for who they were with nothing expected in return, exactly the same as any parent would do for a brand-new baby. That is how you grow a relationship.

Life Lately

Almost fifteen years, eight kids, and lots of life later, I still find infertility waging battles in my heart every now and then. And that's okay. It is a part of my life's story, and I would not trade the experiences, friendships, or lessons learned. Ever! It is a significant part of who I am as a woman and as a mother. Adam and I still believe there is one more adoption out there for us. Many opportunities have come our way, but nothing that has felt right and worked out the way we hoped. Regardless of what comes next for our family, I choose to direct my focus on a faith-filled and purposeful future by living an attitude of gratitude. Our kids are generally bigger than they are little now. We have mostly teens and tweens in the house. Our days are busy, chaotic, and emotionally charged, but also joyful, fun, and everything we hoped for when we embarked on our first adoption adventure.

My children are happy. They are open. They choose the light of the future and our family over the darkness of their pasts. Every single one of them chooses this, so far. They are not perfect. They struggle. They each have weaknesses to overcome and loss to continually reconcile, which puts them on pretty equal footing with the rest of us. We each choose to live in our pasts or live for our futures. We choose our future by the decisions we make today. Nothing worth doing is done for us. We must decide to be happy. And that is so very difficult sometimes. It is difficult in the midst of profound grief and loss. It is difficult when our faith has been shaken by decisions in and out of our control, when putting one foot in front of the other is literally all we can do.

Happy is not just a simple little adjective we use when everything in our day is going right. True joy is a state of being. It is something we are, not just something we feel. And when we can find joy and grace in the midst of those unbearable burdens, which will fall on us all, there we will find our Savior ever smiling right alongside us helping us bear up the burdens that we carry.

We must choose to move forward without bitterness and without regret or we will forever be disappointed. For where there is bitterness, happiness cannot be. William James wrote, "The greatest revolution of our generation is the discovery that human beings, by changing the inner attitudes of their minds, can change the outer aspects of their lives."

Infertility, and subsequently foster care and adoption, laid at my doorstep a grand opportunity for refinement. It changed the landscape of our family in a profound way. And now, all these years later, happiness dwells in the seat of my soul. I have selfish moments still. Many, in fact! However, as I have diligently worked on walking straight through this trial for over a decade now, exposed to emotion and open to being taught, those moments are fewer and farther between.

I have felt the Lord's arm right there on my own shoulder every time I have needed it. Every time a pregnancy slipped through our fingers. Every time an adoption failed or a birth mother chose differently or a foster baby had to be returned or I had a temporary moment of grief and sadness. I have felt Him right there. As I wrap myself up in the warmth of the Savior's light, I experience that state of being, the being of true joy, and gratitude for all He has taught me.

Living gracefully is a lifelong pursuit. The residual effects of infertility, like the loss of a child or spouse, or an intense battle with illness or addiction struggles, never really leave. I am still learning and growing every single day directly because of it. It has not been easy, but I can honestly say I would do it a thousand times over. I would not change a single thing about our family from where we started to where we have landed. I want to be right here, right now, doing what I am doing. Purposefully. Gracefully. Graciously. Every moment has all been worth it, a life full of purpose and faith and grace, all because one day many years ago, on the side of the road, I chose to change my attitude! Our decisions really do determine our destinies.

Charles Swindoll—author and educator—said: "Attitude, to me, is more important than... the past, than money, than circumstances, than failures, than successes, than what other people think or say or do. It is more important than appearance, giftedness, or skill. It will make or break a company, a church, a home. The remarkable thing is we have a choice every day regarding the attitude we will embrace for that day."

It is truly remarkable. Every day we get to choose. Agency, the great gift from the Giver above, allows us to choose and to ever be reaching toward improvement. Young and old, sick and healthy, rich and poor, parents and children, are not we are all in the same place, in the middle of our eternal existence, learning and growing, becoming our very best selves?

Infertility and adoption, working in tandem, have brought the best out in me. They are the birthplace of my family and my personal joy. They contain the moments and experiences that not only made me stronger in the past, but also make life worth living in the present. I am just an everyday, ordinary mom filled with purpose and grace, doing the best I can. And that will always be enough for me. I would not trade my personal trials for anything.

Just like my children, I too am like a kite. As the struggles of life continue to push against me, I find myself lifted off the pavement, sometimes just a few inches, as I shuffle along the sidewalk. Other times, when I allow those struggles to push harder, I am lifted high off the ground as the constant pressure of refinement steadies me in flight. And as I look down from above, I see the chasers below, my children, are the ones helping me to soar.

Epilogue

McCracken Adventures Continue

We continue to cast a wide net in our own lives, and once again it has led somewhere that we did not see from the shore. We are once again getting licensed for foster care in hope of serving another sibling group. Join us at <u>Chasing Kites</u> (<u>https://www.chasingkites.com/</u>)as we create resources and trainings to help all families fly. Join our online community where we build relationships with others and strengthen the relationships in our homes. Our time together may just heal your own heart or possibly open you to a new way of loving.

If anything, we will laugh, we will cry, and we will come out better than we were before.

Chasing Kites

Services
- Online classes for those interested in adoption
- Online training courses for adoption and foster credits
- Online Facebook Community (https://www.facebook.com/chasingkitesfoundation/) for current and prospective adoptive, foster, and blended parents
- Live Hangouts where we answer questions and highlight family stories
- A Publishing Service that helps affordably self-publish stories like Chasing Kites

Coming soon
- Adoption Scholarships for qualifying families
- Online store where you can find gifts for adoptive, foster, and other blended families
- Additional books and resources to help all families fly

Check us Out

www.ChasingKites.com

Thank you so much!

I appreciate you reading my family's story.

A portion of all sales helps fund our foundation, the non-profit arm of <u>Chasing Kites</u>, which supports adoptive and foster families through scholarships and other resources.

You can help support the foundation by leaving a helpful **REVIEW** on <u>AMAZON</u>, <u>GOODREADS</u> or your favorite book distributor.

Like us on Facebook: <u>@chasingkitesfoundation</u>
Follow us on Instagram: <u>@chasingkites_foundation</u>
Join us in our Parent Support Group on FB clicking <u>HERE</u>

Warmest blessings,
~Rachel

The perfect choice for your next
Book Club Read

**Download Your FREE
Discussion Guide Today!**

TO DOWNLOAD GO TO:

https://chasingkites.com/bookguide

www.ChasingKites.com

Acknowledgments

First and foremost, a giant shout-out to my accountability partner, Jennifer L. Gee. Dependable, trustworthy, honest, and kind—the perfect person to encourage me through this project. There is no way I would be this far without her. I am so proud of the content she is providing for parents on her blog at <u>No Perfect Parents Allowed</u>. (http://www.noperfectparentsallowed.com/)

***

Second, a million and one heartfelt thank-yous to my **launch team** which was full of my amazingly loyal family and friends—all of them.

They gave feedback, shared posts, beta read, believed in my abilities, and encouraged me in every way. I am not sure what I ever did to deserve a circle of influence such as this. Thank you!

About the Author

Rachel McCracken is a writer, blogger, and creator of **Chasing Kites**—a business and foundation committed to serving adoptive and foster families. What Rachel finds most rewarding about working with families is the opportunity to connect: "Our fundamental need and formation of attachments is a part of every human experience. Watching tender new connections blossom into deep-rooted relationships is what I love most about serving families."

Rachel is a mom to eight children, seven of whom are adopted. She currently lives in Las Vegas, Nevada, although a part of her heart will always reside at her country farmhouse in central Washington. Over the years, Rachel has helped numerous families navigate the uncertainties and celebrate the joys that come through adoption.

If you would like to hire Rachel for a writing or editing job, or if you are looking for direction within the adoption and self-publishing worlds, please email her: rachel@chasingkites.com

Made in the USA
Monee, IL
20 April 2020